Advanced Test in C
and
Embedded System Programming

Out of Box Knowledge

- One may get an electric shock if an adaptor is attached to the power supply cord fails. So, to avoid this buy laptop/mobile and its charger from authorised dealers, unauthorised chargers are extremely dangerous.
- Many times laptop suck in cooling air (the flow of air into the laptop is disturbed) through their bottoms. If they are placed on an uneven surface like bed, pillow. It causes overheating and thus may result in explosion.
- If laptop is plugged in all the times for charging may explode due to overheating.
- Mishandling of the laptop may lead to its explosion as in case if you drop it somewhere, its battery alignment may get disturbed and results in overheating.
- In hot and humid environment, there are chances of short-circuit that causes overheating and thus explosion of laptop.
- Try to change a laptop battery if it is old with new one and if it is not possible to replace, then remove the battery and run the laptop on direct power supply.
- If you are away on a vacation, do not forget to remove the battery and keep it in a dry place.

Advanced Test in C

and

Embedded System Programming

By

Ashok K. Pathak

BPB PUBLICATIONS

20 ANSARI ROAD, DARYA GANJ, NEW DELHI-110002

REPRINT 2026

REPRINTED 2019

FIRST INDIAN EDITION 2002

Distributors:

COMPUTER BOOK CENTRE12,
Shrungar Shopping Centre,
M.G.Road, BENGALURU–560001
Ph: 25587923/25584641

BPB BOOK CENTRE
376 Old Lajpat Rai Market,
DELHI-110006
Ph: 23861747

DECCAN AGENCIES
4-3-329, Bank Street,
HYDERABAD-500195
Ph: 24756967/24756400

INFOTECH
G-2, Sidhartha Building,
96 Nehru Place,
NEW DELHI-110019
Ph: 26438245

MICRO MEDIA
Shop No. 5, Mahendra Chambers,
150 DN Rd. Next to Capital Cinema,
V.T (C.S.T.)Station, MUMBAI-400001

BPB PUBLICATIONS
20, Ansari Road, Darya Ganj
New Delhi-110002
Ph: 23254990/23254991

LIMITS OF LIABILITY AND DISCLAIMER OF WARRANTY

The Author & Publisher of this book have tried their best to ensure that the programmes, procedures and functions described in the book are correct. However, the author and the publishers make no warranty of any kind, expressed or implied, with regard to these programmes or the documentation contained in the book. The Author and Publishers shall not be liable or consequential, in connection with, or arising out of the furnishing, performance or use purposes only and may trademarks of their respective companies.

ISBN : 81-7656-676-4

Published by Manish Jain for BPB Publications, 20 Ansari Road, Darya Ganj, New Delhi110 002 and Printed by Balaji Printing Press, New Delhi-110020.

Printed at Manipal Technologies Limited, Manipal

To Denis M. Ritchie

Whose suggestion and wishes

Makes this possible

To those

Who really want good of others

Preface

C is popular general purposes programming language. I enjoy programming in it. As in C, I found beginners as well as experienced stumbled. In response to this situation I felt there was a definite need for such a test that could help a C/Embedded programmer to test their programming strength and understanding problem in embedded system programming. The primary aim of this book is to help the C/embedded Programmer to test his programming strength, improve his confidence and leads to mastery.

This book is organized around 300 of the problem with detailed explanation. The book provides an accurate and complete representation of the C programming and RTOS test. The fifteen test are based on the real problem encounter during programming and include every type of question that can be expected in the university/ IT industry interview. Following each test is an answer with detailed explanation designed to clarify the material to the programmers. By completing all fifteen tests and studying the explanations, programmers can discover their strength and weakness in embedded system programming.

Appendix b provides the use of volatile variable that is poorly understood by many programmers as most C texts dismiss it in a few sentences.

Using this book

In the entire test following convention are used

In all program, assume that the required header file/files has /have been included

Consider the data type

- char is 1 byte
- int is 2 byte
- long int 4 byte
- float is 4 byet
- double is 8 byte
- long double is 10 byte
- pointer is 2 byte

$ indicate unix prompt

- Consider all the problem on little endian Machinee

little endian Machine . In little endian Machine the least –significant byte is stored in the lowest –numbered memory address, and the most –significant byte in the highest address. this method is used with Intel family of microprocessor.

Figure I shows how the number 1020h appears when stored in memory location 6000H and 60001H

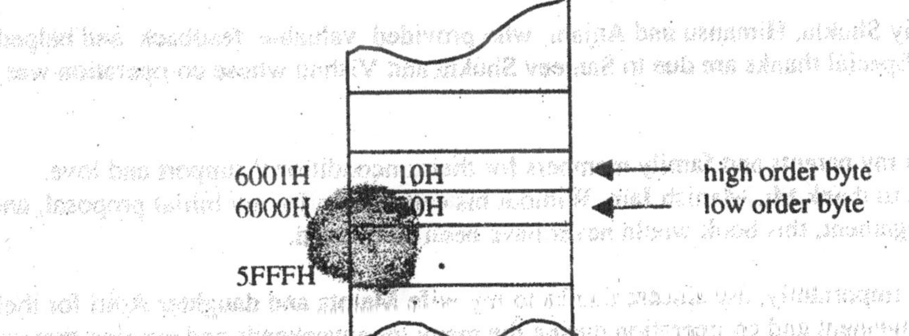

Figure I

Alternate method used in Motorola family of processor, is called the big endian format. in big endian format , number are stored with the lowest location containing the most –significant data

Acknowledgments

Special thanks to
Mr. Denis M. Ritchie
Prof B.D. Chaudhary
For their comments, and suggestions in part or by whole

This book would not been possible without the assistance, comments, and suggestions of many individuals. I am deeply indebted to the following reviewers in part or by whole for theirs valuable comments and suggestion for this manuscript.

Dan Sake	President (Saks & associates USA)
Ashish Nagar	Software Engineer (Intel)
Visal Sisodia	Software engineer (Huges software system)
Vaishali Saxena	Softwrae Engineer (Mistral solution)
Nirmal Pandey	Memebr (Research staff) CRL (BEL)
Sanjeev Shukla	Memebr (Research staff) CRL (BEL)
Ashish Srivastava	Memebr (Research staff) CRL (BEL)
Debasis Biswas	Memebr (Research staff) CRL (BEL)
Deepika Gupta	Memebr (Research staff) CRL (BEL)
G. Srinivas	Memebr (Research staff) CRL (BEL)

Thanks to, Sanjay Shukla, Himansu and Anjani who provided valuable feedback and helped debug the manuscript. Special thanks are due to Sanjeev Shukla and Vishnu whose co-operation was always with me.

I am great full to my parents and family members for their unconditional support and love.
I would also like to thank Mr. Manish Jain. Without his enthusiasm for my initial proposal, and constant encouragement, this book would never have been completed.

Finally and most importantly, my sincere thanks to my wife Mamta and daughter Aditi for their patience, encouragement and co-operation during the many long weekends and evening that went into the writing of this manuscript. Comments about the book are welcome and can be sent by email to **bpb@vsnl.com**

Ashok K.Pathak
August 2002

Contents

Part I
Advanced Test in C

Test 1 1
Answer With Detailed Explanations test 1 11
Test 2 20
Answer with Detailed Explanations test 2 29
Test 3 34
Answer with Detailed Explanations test 3 42
Test 4 48
Answer with Detailed Explanations test 4 56
Test 5 61
Answer with Detailed Explanations test 5 67
Test 6 70
Answer with Detailed Explanations test 6 78
Test 7 82
Answer with Detailed Explanations test 7 91
Test 8 95
Answer with Detailed Explanations test 8 103
Test 9 108
Answer with Detailed Explanations test 9 110
Test 10 112
Answer with Detailed Explanations test 10 114
Test 11 116
Answer with Detailed Explanations test 11 126

Part II
Advanced Test in Embedded System Programming

Test 12 131
Answer with Detailed Explanations test 12 135
Test 13 141
Answer With Detailed Explanations test 13 145
Test 14 148
Answer With Detailed Explanations test 14 153
Test 15 FAQ on Embedded System Programming 156
Appendix a 164
Appendix b 166

C IN DEPTH

Price: Rs. 360/-

ISBN:9788183330480

Pages: 497

Author: Srivastava/ Srivastava

The book explains each topic in depth without compromising over the lucidity of the text and programs. This approach makes this book suitable for both novices and advanced programmers. The well structured programs are easily understandable by the beginners and useful for the experienced programmers. The book can be used as tool for self-study as it provides step by step explanation and comes with solutions of all exercises. It explains all the basic concept and doesn't assume that you know how to program. New features in the 3D edition include a chapter on Recursion, through explanation of Bitwise Manipulation, new and improved programming examples, lots of new exercises ranging in difficulty, solution to all the exercises and a CD includes of all the programming examples and exercises. The book contains about 310 well explained programming examples to drive the concept home and nearly 450 exercises which includes many interesting and challenging programming exercises that will help you to your programming skill. The concept on project development and library creation an help students in implementing their knowledge.

Contents

- ✔ Introduction
- ✔ Elements Of C
- ✔ Input-outout In C
- ✔ Operators And Expressions
- ✔ Control Statements
- ✔ Function
- ✔ Recursion
- ✔ Arrays
- ✔ Pointers
- ✔ Strings
- ✔ Structures And Union
- ✔ Files
- ✔ The C Preprocessor
- ✔ Operation On Bits
- ✔ Miscellaneous Features
- ✔ Building Project And Creation Of Library
- ✔ Code Optimization In C
- ✔ C And Assembly Interaction
- ✔ Library Function

Available at www.bpbonline.com, Amazon, Flipkart, Paytm, and all Leading Book Stores

26082016

Test 1

1. Consider the following program:

```
#include<setjmp.h>
static jmp_buf  buf ;
main( )
{
    volatile  int b;
    b =3 ;
    if(setjmp(buf)!=0)  {
       printf("%d ", b) ;
       exit(0);
    }
    b=5;
    longjmp(buf , 1) ;
}
```

The output for this program is:
(a) 3
(b) 5
(c) 0
(d) None of the above

2. Consider the following program:

```
main( )
{
    struct node {
       int a ;
       int b ;
       int c ;
    } ;
    struct node  s= { 3, 5,6 }  ;
    struct node *pt = &s ;
    printf("%d" ,  *(int*)pt);
}
```

The output for this program is:
(a) 3
(b) 5
(c) 6

(d) 7

3. Consider the following program:

```
void f(char *);
main( )
{
    f("123");
}
void f(char a[])
{
    if(a[1] =='\0') return ;
        f(a+1);
        f(a+1);
        printf("%c ", a[1]);
    }
```

The output for this program is:
(a) 3 2 1
(b) 3 3 3
(c) 3 3 2
(d) 1 2 3

4. Consider the following program:

```
/* tmp.c */
main(int argc , char*argv[] )
{
    if(argc ==1)
    printf("error");
    printf("%c " , *(argv[1] +1));
    printf("%c " , (*(argv+1))[2]);
    printf("%c " , argv[1][2]);
}
```

The output for this program is if input is given as $ tmp 3579
(a) 5 7 7
(b) 5 7 9
(c) 3 5 7
(d) 7 7 9

5. Consider the following program:

```
main( )
{
    unsigned char c;
    typedef struct name {
        long a;
        int b ;
        long c;
    }r ;
    r re = { 3,4,5};
    r *na= &re;
    printf("%d" ,*(int*) ((char*)na +  (unsigned int) & ( (
    (struct name *)0 )->b) ) )    ;
}
```

The output for this program is:

(a) 3
(b) 4
(c) 5
(d) 6

6. Consider the following code segment:

```
int foo ( int x , int n)
{
    int val ;
    val =1;
    if (n>0) {
    if (n%2 == 1) val = val *x;
        val = val * foo(x*x , n/2) ;
    }

}
```

What function of x and n is compute by this code segment?

(a) x^n
(b) x*n
(c) n^x
(d) None of the above

7. Consider the following program:

```
void  foo(int a ,int b ,...);
main( )
{
```

```
    foo(1,5);
    foo(2,5,6);
}
void foo( int a,int b, ...)
{
    int j ;
    int *ptr = &b ;
    j=0 ;
    while(j<a) {
    printf("%d " , *ptr);
    ++j ;
    ++ptr ;
    }
}
```

The output for this program is:

(a) 5 5 6
(b) 1 5 2 5 6
(c) 1 2
(d) None of the above

8. Consider the following program:

```
char i;
void try1();
void try2( char*);
main( )
{
   try1();
}
void try1( )
{
   static char *ptr = "abcde" ;
   i =*ptr ;
   printf("%c" , i);
   try2(++ptr) ;
}
void try2(char *t)
{
   static char *pt;
   pt = t + strlen(t)-1 ;
   if(i!=*pt--)
   if(t!=pt)
```

```
    try1();
}
```

The output for this program is:
(a) ab
(b) abcd
(c) abc
(d) abcde

9. Consider the following program:

```
main( )
{
    int  a[5] = {1,2,3,4,5};
    int *ptr =  (int*)(&a+1);
    printf("%d %d" , *(a+1), *(ptr-1) );

}
```

The output for this program is:
(a) 2 2
(b) 2 1
(c) 2 5
(d) None of the above

10. Consider the following program:

```
main( )
{
    double a[2][3] ;
    printf("%d " ,  sizeof(a));
    printf("%d " ,  sizeof(a[1]));
    printf("%d " ,  sizeof(a[1][1]));
}
```

The output for this program is:
(a) 48 8 8
(b) 48 48 48
(c) 40 40 8
(d) 48 24 8

11. Consider the following program:

```
void foo(int [][3] );
main( )
```

```
{
    int a [3][3]= { { 1,2,3} , { 4,5,6},{7,8,9}};
    foo(a);
    printf("%d" , a[2][1]) ;
}
void foo( int b[][3])
{
    ++ b;
    b[1][1] =9 ;
}
```

The output for this program is:
(a) 8
(b) 9
(c) 7
(d) None of the above

12. Consider the following program:

```
main( )
{
   union  {
      struct{
         char c[2] ;
         char ch[2];
      }s;
      struct  {
         int i;
         int j ;
      }st;

   } u = { {12 ,1} , {15 , 1}} ;

   printf("%d %d", u.st.i , u.st.j) ;
}
```

The output for this program is:
(a) 15 12
(b) 268 271
(c) 12, 15
(d) None of the above

13. Consider the following program:

```
main( )
{
   struct {
      char a[11] ;
      int  i;
   }st= { "done" , 10 } ;
   printf("%s" , (&st)->a);
   printf("%d" , (&st)->i);
}
```

The output for this program is:
(a) done 10
(b) undefined undefined
(c) 0 0
(d) Not compile

14. Consider the following program:

```
main( )
{
   char *ptr;
   ptr = strtok("jan:feb,mar", ":");
   printf(ptr);
   do {
   ptr = strtok('\0', ":");
   if(ptr) printf(" %5s ", ptr);
   } while(ptr);
}
```

The output for this program is:
(a) jan feb,mar
(b) jan feb mar
(c) jan:feb,mar
(d) None of the above

15. Consider the following program:

```
main( )
{
   int a, b,c, d;
   a=3;
   b=5;
   c=a,b;
   d=(a,b);
```

```
    printf("c=%d" ,c);
    printf("d=%d" ,d);
}
```

The output for this program is:
(a) c=3 d=3
(b) c=5 d=3
(c) c=3 d=5
(d) c=5 d=5

16. Consider the following program:

```
struct st {
    int a ;
    int b ;
} ;
void foo( struct st *);
main()
{
    struct st ab = { 128 , 768} ;
    struct st *pq =&ab;
    foo(pq);
}
void foo(struct st *p)
{
    char *pt;
    p->a =768;
    p->b =128;
    pt= (char*)p ;
    printf("%d" ,*++pt) ;
}
```

The output for this program is:
(a) 1
(b) 2
(c) 3
(d) 4

17. Consider the following program:

```
main( )
{
```

```
    int a[][3] = { 1,2,3 ,4,5,6};
    int (*ptr)[3] =a ;
    printf("%d %d "   ,(*ptr)[1], (*ptr)[2] );
    ++ptr;
    printf("%d %d"   ,(*ptr)[1], (*ptr)[2] );
}
```

The output for this program is:
(a) 2 3 5 6
(b) 2 3 4 5
(c) 4 5 0 0
(d) None of the above

18. Consider following function

```
int *f1(void)
{
int x =10 ;
return(&x);
}
int *f2(void)
{
    int*ptr ;
    *ptr =10;
    return ptr;
}
int *f3(void)
{
    int *ptr;
    ptr=(int*) malloc(sizeof(int));
    return ptr;
}
```

Which of the above three functions are likely to cause problem with pointers
(a) Only f3
(b) Only f1 and f3
(c) Only f1 and f2
(d) f1 , f2 ,f3

19. Consider the following statement:
s1 : An operator may require an lvalue operand , yet yield an rvalue
s2 : An operator may accept an rvalue operand , yet gives an lvalue
Which of the following is true about s1 and s2
(a) Both s1 and s2 are correct

(b) Only s1 is correct
(c) Only s2 is correct
(d) Both s1 and s2 are incorrect

20. Consider the following program:

```
main( )
{
    int i=3;
    int j;
    j = sizeof(++i+ ++i);
    printf("i=%d j=%d", i ,j);
}
```

The output for this program is:
(a) i=4 j=2
(b) i=3 j=2
(c) i=3 j=4
(d) i=3 j=6

Answers With Detailed Explanations

Test 1

1. (b)
volatile variable isn't affected by the optimization. Its value after the longjump is the last value variable assumed. b last value is 5 hence 5 is printed.
setjmp : Sets up for nonlocal goto /* setjmp.h*/
Stores context information such as register values so that the lomgjmp function can return control to the statement following the one calling setjmp.Returns 0 when it is initially called.
Lonjjmp: longjmp Performs nonlocal goto /* setjmp.h*/
Transfers control to the statement where the call to setjmp (which initialized buf) was made. Execution continues at this point as if longjmp cannot return the value 0;
A nonvolatile automatic variable might be changed by a call to longjmp. When you use setjmp and longjmp, the only automatic variables guaranteed to remain valid are those declared volatile.
Note: Test program without volatile qualifier (result may very) see also appendix B

2. (a)
The members of structures have address in increasing order of their declaration. If a pointer to a structure is cast to the type of a pointer to its first member, the result refers to the first member.

3. (c)

4.

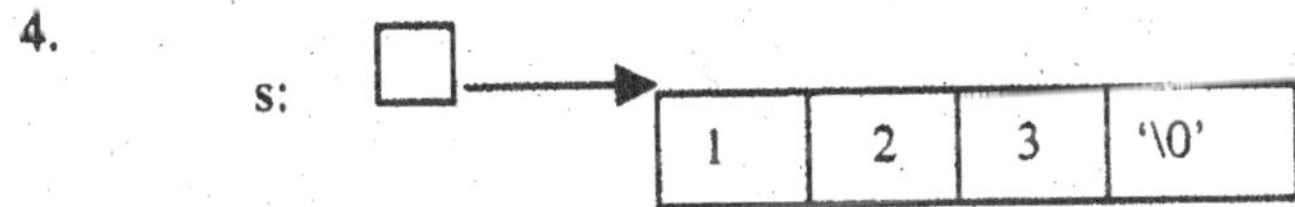

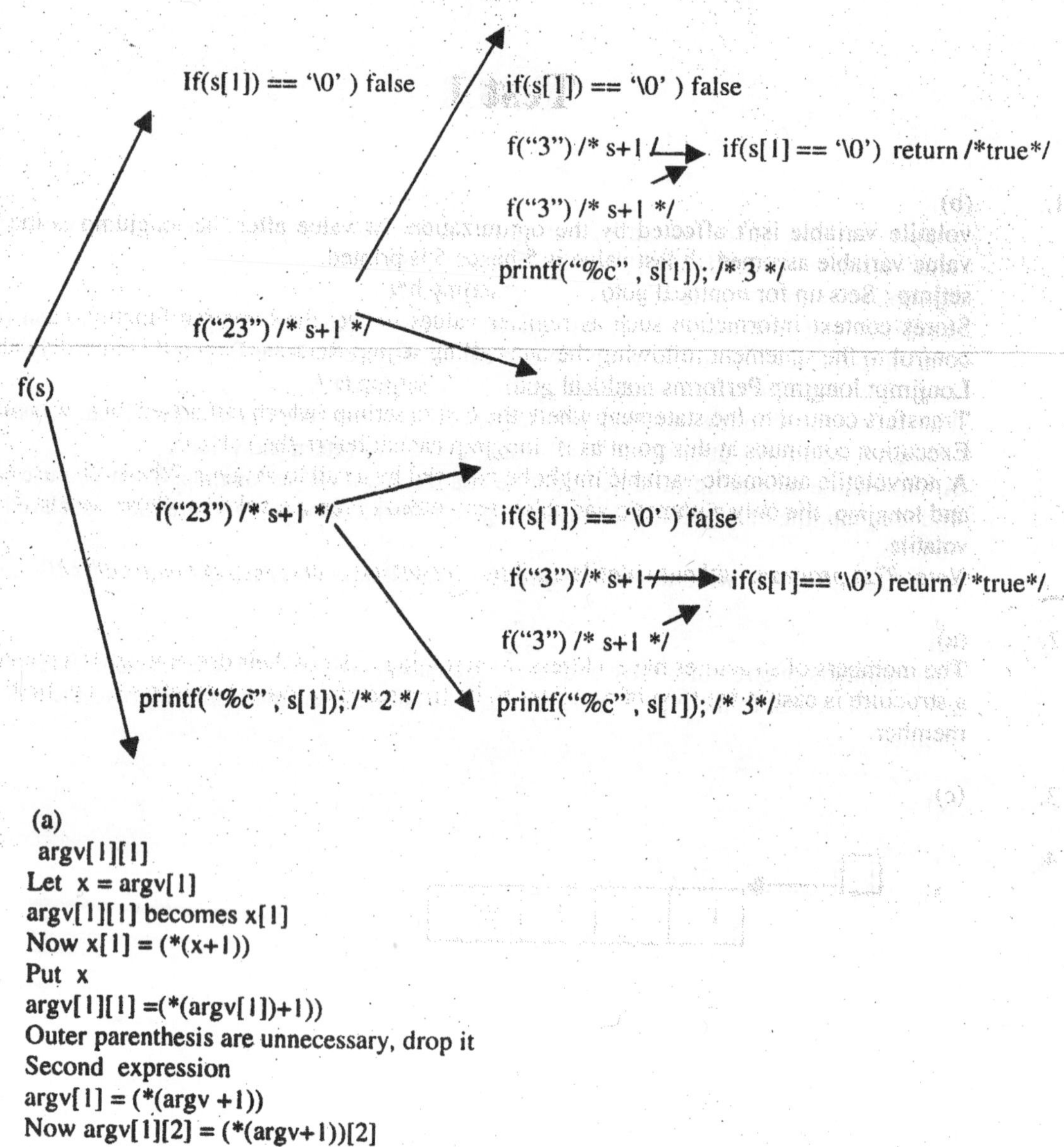

4. (a)

argv[1][1]
Let x = argv[1]
argv[1][1] becomes x[1]
Now x[1] = (*(x+1))
Put x
argv[1][1] =(*(argv[1])+1))
Outer parenthesis are unnecessary, drop it
Second expression
argv[1] = (*(argv +1))
Now argv[1][2] = (*(argv+1))[2]

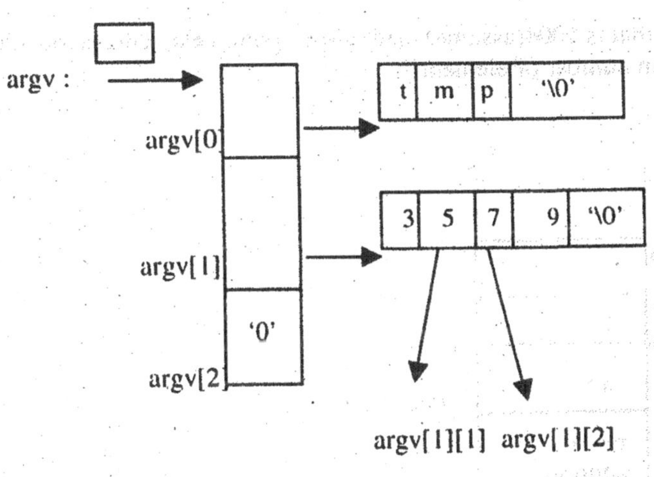

5. (b)
Null pointer is converted is supposed to guarantee that a simple offset(of a structure) is computed. cast to (char*) insure that offset so computed is a byte offset

6. (a)
Non recursive version of the program

```
int  what ( int x , int  n)
{
    int val ;
    int product ;
    product -1;
    val =x;
    while(n>0)   {
    if (n%2 == 1)   product = product*val;
       n = n/2;
       val - val* val ;
    }
}
```

/* Code raise a number (x) to a large power (n) using binary doubling strategy */
Algorithm description
(while n>0) {
if next most significant binary digit of n(power) is one
then multiply accumulated product by current val ,
reduce n(power) sequence by a factor of two using integer division .

get next val by multiply current value of itself

}

7. (a)

ptr contain addres of b that is 1004(assume) and ++ptr point next address too 1006 and so on /*while(j<a) a contain number of element */

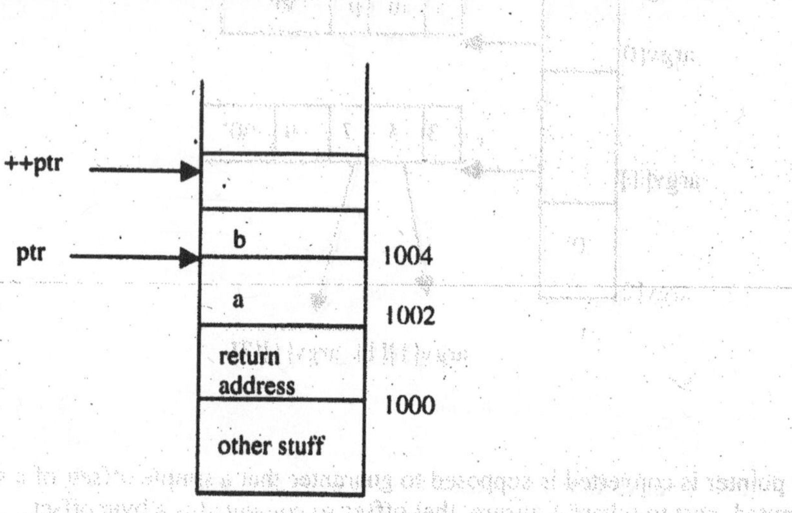

8. (c)

```
in try1( )
{
    .
    .

    printf("%c" , i);   /* print  a **/
    try2(++ptr)

}
```

figure show variable and pointer point after call for try2

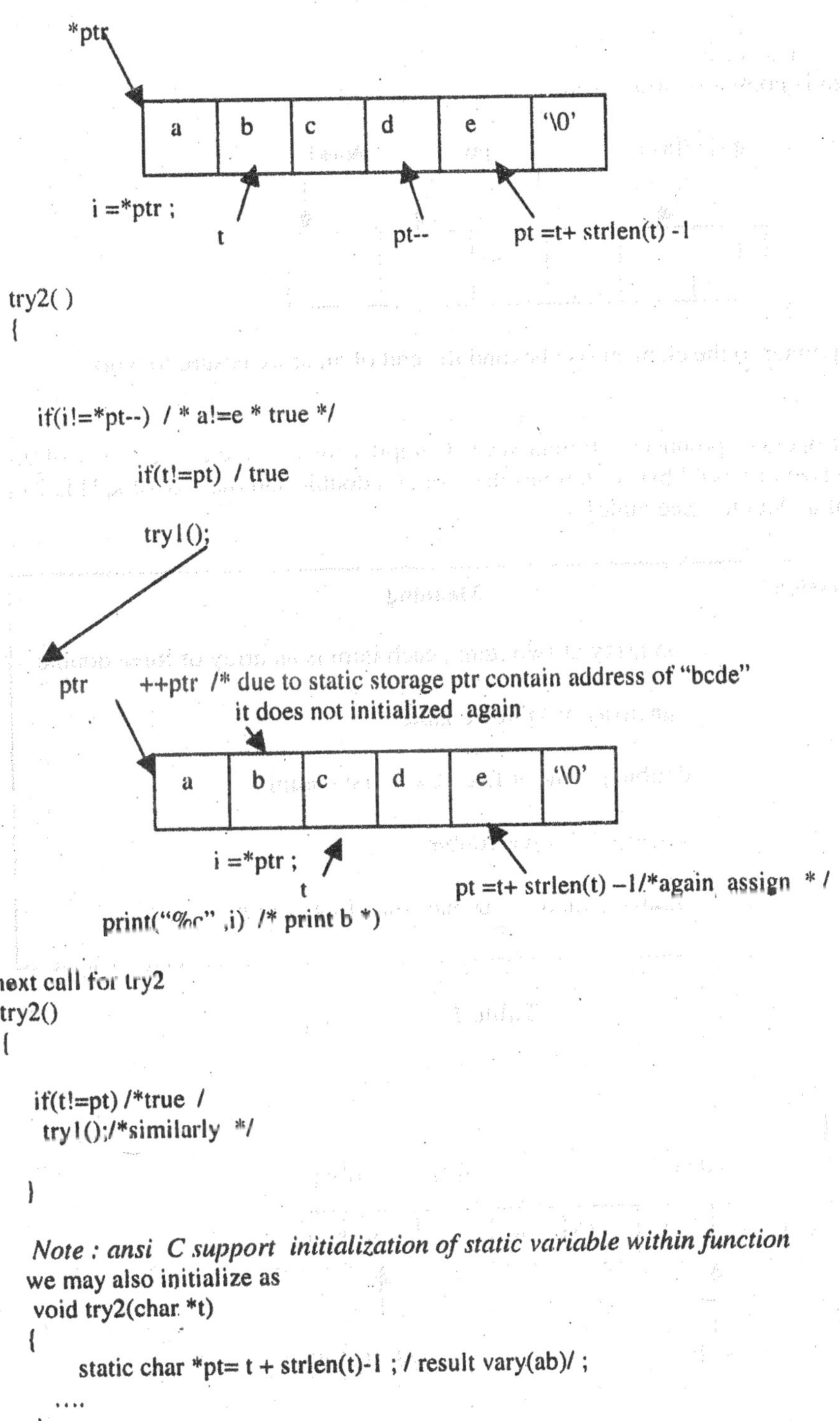
*ptr
a
b
c
d
e
'\0'
i =*ptr ;
t
pt--
pt =t+ strlen(t) -1
try2( )
{
if(i!=*pt--) / * a!=e * true */
if(t!=pt) / true
try1();
ptr
++ptr /* due to static storage ptr contain address of "bcde"
it does not initialized again
a
b
c
d
e
'\0'
i =*ptr ;
t
pt =t+ strlen(t) –1/*again assign * /
print("%c" ,i) /* print b *)
next call for try2
try2()
{
if(t!=pt) /*true /
try1();/*similarly */
}
Note : ansi C support initialization of static variable within function
we may also initialize as
void try2(char *t)
{
static char *pt= t + strlen(t)-1 ; / result vary(ab)/ ;
....
}

9. (c)
type of a is array of int
type of &a is pointer to array of int

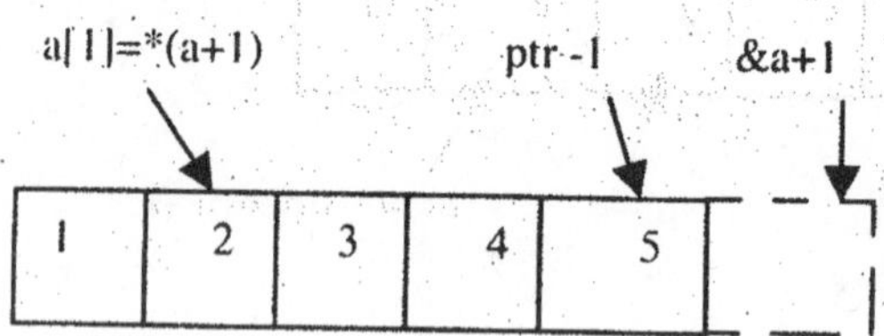

Taking a pointer to the element one beyond the end of an array is sure to work.

10. (d)
The sizeof operator produces different sizes. Compiler treats a and a[1] as array of different sizes. The size of a is 48 bytes (6 times the size of a double and the size of a[1] is 24 (3 time the size of a double).See table1

Expression	Meaning
a	an array of two item , each item is an array of three double
*a	an array of three double
**a	double , value at first row , first column
a[1]	an array of three double
*a[1]	double , value at second row , first column

Table 1

11. (b)

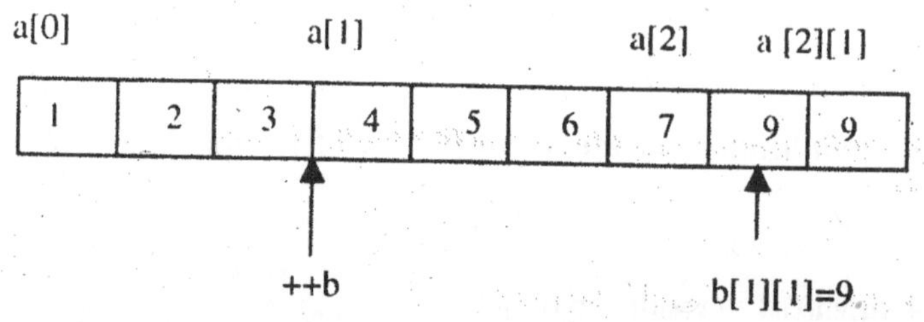

For passing a two dimensional array to a function
The function declaration must match
foo(int [][3]) /* array of array decay to pointer to array)
in multidimensional array only first dimension may be missing */
foo((*a) [3]);

12 (b)

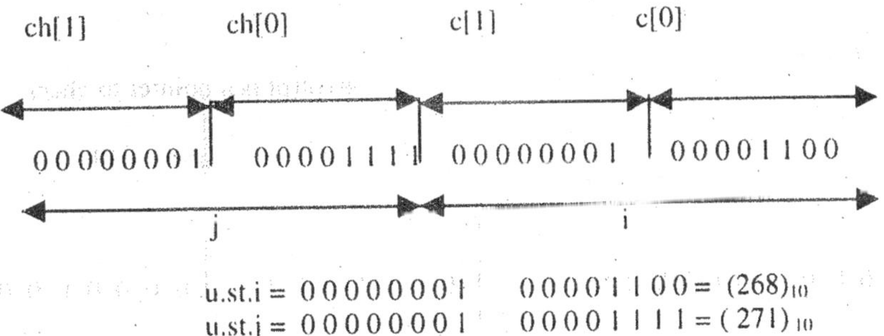

u.st.i = 00000001 00001100 = $(268)_{10}$
u.st.j = 00000001 00001111 = $(271)_{10}$

13. (a)
(&st) is a pointer (&st)-> read the member

14. (a)
char strtok(char s1, const char s2); /* string.h */
strtok scans s1 for the first token not contained in s2
s2 defines separator characters(in this case :). strtok interprets the string s1 as a series of tokens separated by spans of characters in s2(in this program :).If no tokens are found in s1, returns NULL. If the token is found, a null character is written into s1 following the token, and strtok returns a pointer to the token. Subsequent calls to strtok with NULL as the first argument use the previous s1 string, starting after the last token found.
"jan:feb,mar" /* only two token jan and feb,mar */
"jan:feb:mar" /for this string three token jan feb mar */

15. (c)
The comma separates the elements of a function argument list. The comma is also used as an operator in comma expressions. Mixing the two uses of comma is legal, but you must use parentheses to distinguish them. the left operand E1 is evaluated as a void expression, then E2 is evaluated to give the result and type of the comma expression. By recursion, the expression
E1, E2, ..., En
results in the left-to-right evaluation of each Ei, with the value and type of En giving the result of the whole expression.
c=a,b; / *yields c=a* /
d=(a,b); /* d =b */

16. (c)

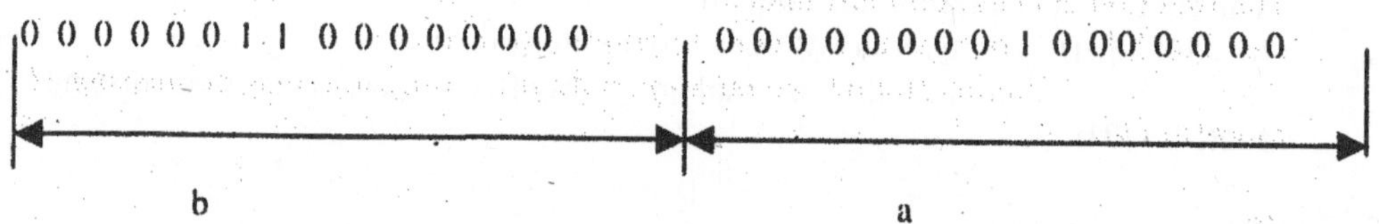

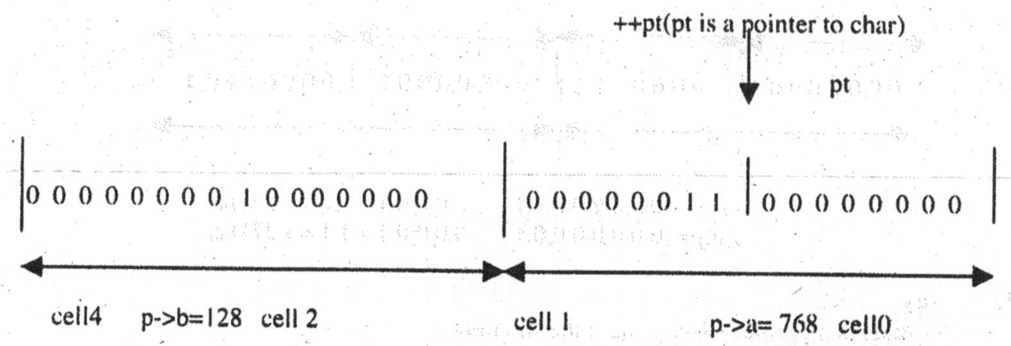

17 (a)

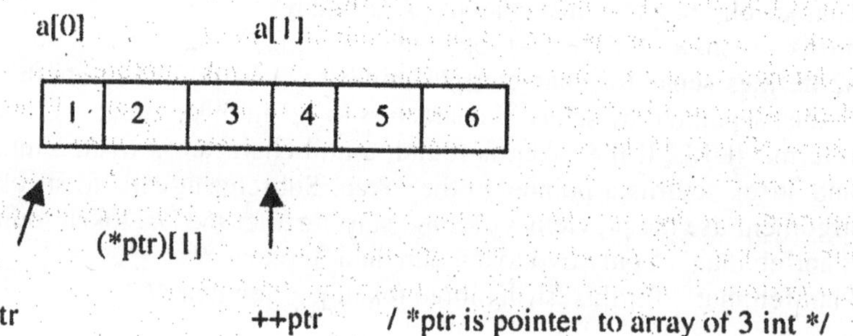

18 (c)

f1 and f2 return address of local variable ,when function exit local variable disappeared

19. (a)

& is one such operator

```
int n;
&n =p      /* is not allowed */
*n  is lvalue
&n is  rvalue
```

operator	operand	result
&	n is lvalue	&n rvalue

```
int a[2]
int *p = a;
p =3 ;          /* ok */
*(p+1) = 5;     /* ok */
```

operator	operand	result
*	(p+1) is rvalue	*(p+1) lvalue

20. (b)
sizeof operator gives the number of bytes required to store an object of the type of its operand . The operands is either an expression, which is not evaluated ((++i + ++ i) is not evaluated so i remain 3 and j is *sizeof* int that is 2)or a parenthesized type name.

Test 2

1. Consider the following program:

```
void f1(int *, int);
void f2(int *, int);
void(*p[2]) ( int *, int) ;
main( )
{
    int a ;
    int b ;
    p[0] = f1 ;
    p[1] = f2;
    a=3;
    b=5;
    p[0](&a , b);
    printf("%d\t %d\t" , a ,b);
    p[1](&a , b);
    printf("%d\t %d\t" , a ,b);
}
void f1( int* p , int q)
{
    int tmp ;
    tmp =*p;
    *p = q ;
    q= tmp ;
}
void f2( int* p , int q)
{
    int tmp ;
    tmp =*p;
    *p = q ;
    q= tmp ;
}
```

The output for this program is:

(a) 5 5 5 5
(b) 3 5 3 5
(c) 5 3 5 3
(d) 3 3 3 3

2. Consider the following program:

```
main( )
{
    char *ptr1 ="abcdef";
       ptr1 = ptr1 +(strlen(ptr1)-1);
       printf("%c" , --*ptr1--);
       printf("%c" , --*--ptr1);
       printf("%c" , --*(ptr1--));
       printf("%c" , --*(--ptr1));
       printf("%c" , *ptr1);
}
```

The output for this program is
(a) ecbaa
(b) edcbb
(c) fedaa
(d) ecdbb

3. Consider the following program:

```
void  e(int );
main( )
{
    int a;
    a=3;
    e(a);
}
void  e(int n)
{
    if(n>0)  {
        e(--n);
        printf("%d" , n);
        e(--n);
    }
}
```

The output for this program is:
(a) 0 1 2 0
(b) 0 1 2 1
(c) 1 2 0 1
(d) 0 2 1 1

4. Consider the following program:

```
main( )
{
    int q, i, j, count;
    i=j=0 ;
    q=2;
    count =6 ;
    switch(3)   {
       case 0 :
       while(--count>0) {
       case 1:
       ++j ;
       case 2:
       ++i;
       case 3: ;
       case 4:;
       case 5: ;
       }
    }
   printf("%d " , i);
   printf("%d " , j);
}
```

The output for this program is:
(a) 3 3
(b) 5 5
(c) 6 6
(d) 1 1

5. Consider the following program:

```
main( )
{
   char  a[]= "abcde";
   char * p= a;
   p++;
   p++;
   p[2]='z';
   printf("%s", p) ;
}
```

The output for this program is:

(a) cde
(b) zde
(c) cdz
(d) abzec

6. Consider the following program:

```
void t1(char* );
main( )
{
    char * p ;
    p ="abcder";
    t1(p);
}
void t1(char  *q)
{
    if(*q!='r')  {
    putchar(*q);
    t1(q++);
    }
}
```

The output for this program is:
(a) abcde
(b) abcder
(c) Stack-overflow;
(d) abc

7. Consider the following program:

```
main( )
{
    char *m[] = {"jan    "feb" "mar" };
    char d[][10] = {"sun", "mon"   "tue" } ;
    printf("%s\t" , m[1]);
    printf("%s" , d[1]);
}
```

The output for this program is:
(a) feb mon
(b) febmar montue
(c) febmarmontue
(d) Not compile

8. Consider the following program:

```
static  unsigned char h[5]={1,2,3,4,5};
main( )
{
    struct ad {
        unsigned short a;
        unsigned  short b;
    };
    struct ad *it;
    it = (struct ad*) h;
    printf("%d ", it->a);
    printf("%d ",it->b);
}
```

The output for this program is:
(a) 513 1027
(b) 1 2
(c) 1027 513
(d) 512 1026

9. Consider the following program:

```
main( )
{
    printf("%d ", sizeof(65555));
    printf("%d ", sizeof(65555L));
    printf("%d ", sizeof(6.5F));
    printf("%d ", sizeof(6.5));
    printf("%d ", sizeof(6.5L));
}
```

The output for this program is:
(a) 2 4 4 8 10
(b) 2 2 4 8 10
(c) 4 4 4 8 10
(d) 4 4 4 4 8

10. main(int argc , char*argv[]) is same as
(a) main(int argc , char**argv[])
(b) main(int argc , char**argv)
(c) main(int argc , char(*argv)[]);
(d) None of the above

11. Consider the following program:

```
#include<stdarg.h>
main( )
{
    int c,d,e,f;
    int a[12]={1,2,3,4,5,6,7,8,9,10,11} ;
    int *p =a;
       c =va_arg(p,int);
       d =va_arg(p,int);
       e =va_arg(p,int);
       f =va_arg(p,int);
       printf("c=%d d=%d e=%d f=%d",c,d,e,f);
}
```

The output for this program is:
(a) c=2 d=4 e=6 f=8
(b) c=1 d=2 e=3 f=4
(c) c=3 d=6 e=9 f=11
(d) c=2 d=3 e=4 f=5

12. Consider following declaration

typedef int (*test) (float * , float*)
test tmp ;
type of tmp is

(a) Pointer to function of having two arguments that is pointer to float
(b) Int
(c) Pointer to function having two argument that is pointer to float and return int
(d) None of the above

13. Consider the following program:

```
main( )
{
    char *p ;
    char buf[10] ={ 1,2,3,4,5,6,9,8}
    p = (buf+1)[5]   ;
    printf("%d" , p) ;
}
```

The output for this program is:
(a) 5

(b) 6
(c) 9
(d) None of the above

14. Consider the following program:

```
main( )
{
    char *table [] = { "jan" , "feb" , "march"};
    char **ptr =&table[1];
    printf("%c" ,   (*++*--ptr));
}
```

The output for this program is:
(a) f
(b) a
(c) j
(d) None of the above

15. Which one is the correct declaration of argument in following function?

```
fun(int a[][5])
{

}
fun1(int b[3][5])
{

}
fun2(int c[5][])
{
}
fun3(int d[][])
{

}
```

(a) a b c d
(b) Only a b
(c) Only c d
(d) None of the above

16. Consider the following program:

```
main( )
```

```
{
   float a[10][10];
   float *p , *q;
   unsigned int nu ;
   p=&a[5][8];
   q=&a[10][9];
   if((p-q) > 0 ) nu = p-q ;
   else nu = -( p-q) ;
   printf("%d",nu );
}
```

The output for this program is:
(a) 51
(b) Difference of address of p and q
(c) 15
(d) Pointer subtraction is not allowed

17. Consider the following program:

```
main( )
{
   float a[10][10];
   float *p , *q;
   float *e, *f ;
   p=&a[5][8];
   q=&a[10][9];
   e = p-q + a; / * exp1  */
   f = a + p-q ; /*  exp2  */
}
```

Which one is the right expression?
(a) Only exp1 is right
(b) Only exp2 is right
(c) Both 1 and 2 are right
(d) Neither 1 nor 2 is right

18. Consider the following program:

```
main( )
{
   int a,b;
   a=3;
   b=5;
   a^= b;
```

```
    b^= a;
    a^= b;
}
```

What does the following program do?
(a) Subtract b from a
(b) Swap a and b
(c) Complement a and b
(d) Subtract b from a

19. Which one of the following is false?
(a) A string has type "array of characters"
(b) A string has storage class static
(c) Adjacent string literal are concatenated into a Single string
(d) Concatenation of ordinary and wide string literal is a single string.

20. Consider the following program:

```
main( )
{
    printf("ABCDE"+sizeof("ABC"));
}
```

The output for this program is:
(a) D
(b) Error
(c) E
(d) ABCDE

Answer With Detailed Explanations

Test 2

1. (a)
void(*p[2]) (int *, int) ; define array of pointer to function accept two argument that is pointer to int and return int. p[0] = f1 ; p[1] = f2 contain address of function .function name without parenthesis represent address of function
Value and address of variable is passed to function only argument that is effected is a (address is passed). Because of call by value f1, f2 can not effect b

2. (a)

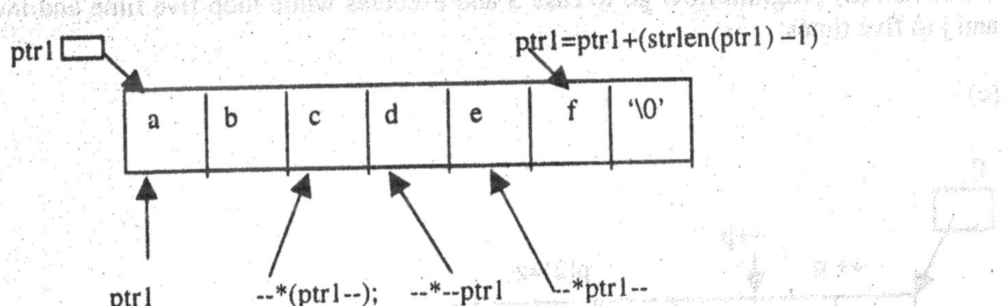

--*ptr1-- print the decrement value what ptr1 points to(ptr1 points to f , decrement f) then decrement ptr , now point to (e)
--*--ptr1 decrement ptr1 then decrement the value ptr1 point to and print (c)
--*(ptr1--)); decrement ptr1 then decrement the value ptr1 point to and print that value (b)
--*(--ptr1)); decrement ptr1 then decrement the value that ptr1 point to and print the value(a)
*ptr1 print the value that ptr1 point to

3. (a)

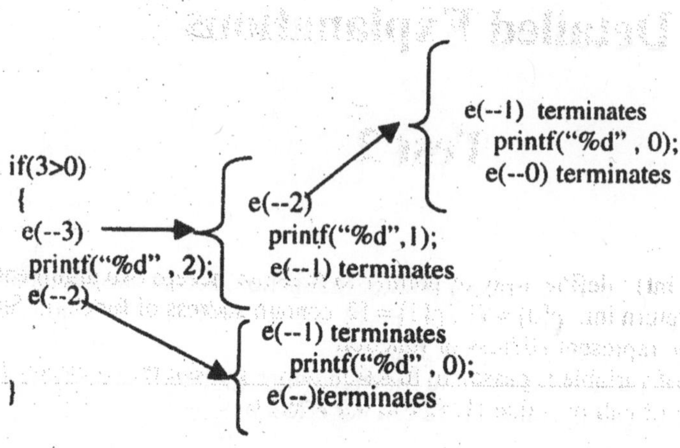

4. (b)
On switch (3) program flow go to case 3 and executes while loop five time and increment i and j to five times.

5. (c)

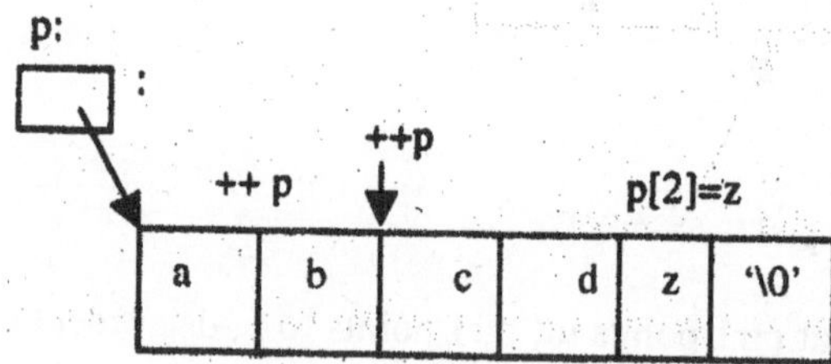

6. (c)

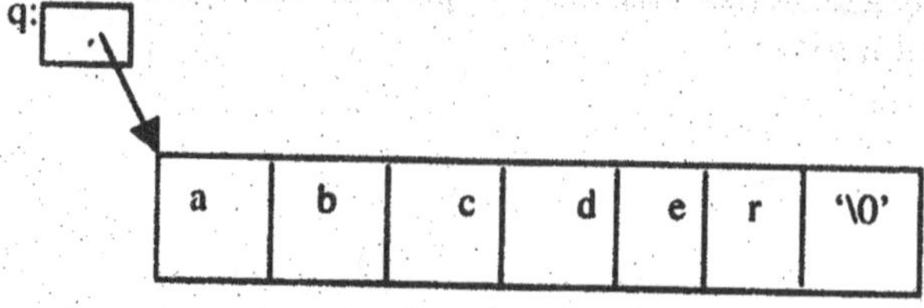

After each call same address will be passes to t1 (q) then address is incremented, q always contain initial address hence stack overflow/ *correct t1(++q) */

7. (b)
"feb" "mar" becomes "febmar"
"mon" "tue" becomes "montue"
m[1] contains address of "febmar"
d[1] contains address of "montue"

8. (a)

h[4]	h[3]	h[2]	h[1]	h[0]
5	4	3	2	1

After type cast with struct ad
a is two byte
b is two byte

h[1] h[0]
it->a is $(00000010\ 00000001)_2 = (513)_{10}$

h[4] h[3]
it->b is $(00000100\ 00000011)_2 = (1027)_{10}$

9. (c)
The type of an integer constant depends on its form (decimal, hex, octal), value, an suffix(l , L , u, U). If it is unsuffixed decimal, it has the first of following types in which its value can be represented
int
long int
unsigned long int

(65555) type is long int because it can not be represented in int (range +32767 , -32767)
(65555L) type is long int because L suffixes it
sizeof(6.5F) float type is determined by the suffix F , or f makes float that is 4 byte
sizeof(6.5) it is double
sizeof(6.5L)l or L make it long double 10 byte

10. (b)

11. (b)
p is a pointer to int object each call of va_arg returns one arguments and steps p to next va_arg uses a type name to determine what type to return and how big a step to take.

12. (c)
C provide a facility called typedef for creating new data type names, for example declaration
typedef char string

Makes the name string a synonym for int .The type string can be used in declaration, cast, etc, exactly the same way that the type int can be. Notice that the type being declared in a typedef appears in the position of a variable name not after the word typedef.

13. (c)
If the type of an expression is "array of T" for some type T, then the value of the expression is a pointer to the first object in the array, and the type of the expression is altered to "pointer to T"
So (buf+1)[5] is equvalent to *(buf +6) or buf[6]

14. (b)

15. (b)
For a multidimensional array, only the first dimension may be missing.
Consider

```
A[][6]
In conversion a[3][5] to
( &a[0][0] + 6*5 + 3 ) // size of  first dimension is not required
```

16. (a)
Pointers to successive objects differ by 1. The value is not defined if the pointers not point to objects within the same array.

17. (a)
Additive operators + and – group left – to –right
Consider first expression
(p-q) + a; / * left to right grouping */
Subtraction of pointer points to same object are allowed
a pointer to an object in an array and a value of any integral type may be added
(a + p)-q /* addition of pointers is not allowed */

18. (b)
Swap a and b

```
        a=3  ; b=5;
a    00000000 00000011
b    00000000 00000101
--------------------------
a= a^b 00000000 000110

now
a    00000000 00000110
b    00000000 00000101
--------------------------
b= b^a 00000000 00000001
```

a 00000000 00000 110
b 00000000 00000011

b= a^b 00000000 0000101

19. (d)
Concatenation of ordinary and wide string literal is undefined
A string has type "array of characters" and storage class static (store in data or code area depend on implementation),
Adjacent string literal is concatenated into single example: string "abc" "def" is concatenated to abcdef".

20 (c)
sizeof ("ABC") yields 4
" ABCDE" +4 = "ABCDE"[4] = E
"ABCDE" is "array of char" this is usually modified to "pointer to char " and the result is a pointer to the first character in the string

Test 3

1. Which one of the following is true about run-time memory organization for C?
   (a) Generally data area contains static variables (internal and external) as well As global variable
   (b) Data area contains only static variable external
   (c) Data area contains only global variable
   (d) Data area contains only static variable internal (local to function)

2. Consider the following program:

```
Void f(char**);
main( )
{
    char * argv[] = { "ab" ,"cd" , "ef" ,"gh", "ij" ,"kl" };
    f( argv );
}
void f( char **p )
{
    char* t ;
    t= (p+= sizeof(int))[-1];
    printf( "%s" , t) ;
}
```

The output for this program is:
(a) ab
(b) cd
(c) ef
(d) gh

3. Compiler uses memory from the data area for the following items:
   (a) Internal and external static variable
   (b) Global variable
   (c) Constant string
   (d) All of the above

4. Consider the following program:

```
Static int a;
char b[10];
struct st {
    float x, y ;
} pt ;
```

```
main( )
{
   static float v []= { 1.2  1.3 };
   static struct st  pt1;
   printf(" %f %f" , v[1] , v[2]) ;
}
```

Which one of the following is true?
(a) Except v all variable reside in bss
(b) All variable reside in bss
(c) Only v reside in bss
(d) No variable reside in bss

5. What does C not contain in stack at run time memory organization?
(a) Automatic variable
(b) Internal static (local to function) variable
(c) Return address of function
(d) Function parameter

6. Consider the following program:

```
main( )
{
   struct ab {
      char *a;
      int b;
      int c;
         };
   struct ab y ={"547895",5,6};
   struct ab *p =&y ;
   printf("++p->a=%s\n", ++p->a);
   printf("*p->a++=%c\n", *p->a++);
   printf("(*p->a)++=%c\n", (*p->a)++);
}
```

The output for this program is:
(a) ++p->a=547895
*p->a++=5
(*p->a)++=6
(b) ++p->a=47895
*p->a++=4
(*p->a)++=7
(c) ++p->a=547895
*p->a++=4

(*p->a)++=8
(d) ++p->a=7895
*p->a++=4
(*p->a)++=9

7. Consider following two code segment in C

```
process1( int counter)
{
   if(counter==1){
   char buf[80] ;
 ........
   }
}
process2( int counter)
{
   char buf [80];
   if(counter==1)
{
.......
}
}
```

Which one is true for above code segment?

(a) both process require same stack space in all case
(b) Process1 require more stack space
(c) Process2 require more stack space
(d) Stack space for process not allocate if counter == 1

Consider the following program:

```
main( )
{
   int i, j, k;

   i =10;
   j=5;
   k=0;
   k= (++i) >(++j) ?(i++):(j++);
   printf("i=%d j= %d k=%d", i , j, k);
}
```

The output for this program is:

(a) i=12 j= 6 k=11
(b) i=12 j= 5 k=12
(c) i=12 j= 6 k=11
(d) i=12 j= 6 k=12

9. Consider the following program:

```
void f(int a, ...) ;
main( )
{
   f(4,10,20,30,40,50);
}
void f(int a,...)
{
   int i;
   int *j=&a ;
   for(i=0 ; i<= a ; i++) {
      ++j;
      printf("%d\n", *j);
   }
}
```

The output for this program is:
(a) 10, 20,30,40,50,
(b) 20,30,40,50
(c) 4,10,20,30,40,50
(d) None of the above

10. Consider the following program:

```
main( )
{
   unsigned a=65545;
   unsigned b=65545;
   unsigned c=a+b;
   printf("%u",c);
}
```

The output for this program is:
(a) 17
(b) 18
(c) Overflow
(d) None of the above

11. Consider the following program:

```
#include<stdarg.h>
int ripple ( int , ...);
main( )
{
    int num ;
    num = ripple ( 3, 5,7);
    printf( " %d" , num) ;
}
int ripple (int n, ...)
{
    int i , j  ;
    int k ;
    va_list p ;
    k= 0;
    j = 1;
    va_start( p , n) ;
    for (  ; j<n ;  ++j) {
    i =  va_arg( p , int) ;
    for ( ; i ;    i &=i-1  )
    ++k;
    }
    return k ;
}
```

The output for this program is:
(a) 7
(b) 6
(c) 5
(d) 3

12. Consider the following program:

```
main( )
{
    int  i , j ;
    i=1;
    j=1;

    while( i ^j || i-- || --j)
    printf( " %d %d" ,i, j );
}
```

The output for this program is:
(a) 0 1
(b) 1 0
(c) 0 0
(d) None of the above

13. Consider the following program:

```
main( )
{
   int i,argc;
   i=argc =3;

   char *arg[3]= { "abcde", "fghij" , "klmno"};
   char **argv=arg;
   while(++argv, --argc,--i)
   printf("%s\n", *argv );
}
```

The output for this program is:
(a) Infinite loop
(b) Abcde
fghij
klmno
(c) fghij
klmno
(d) fghij

14. Consider the following program:

```
main( )
{
   int a[2];
   a[1] =3;
   printf("a[1]=%d " , a[1]);
   printf("1[a]=%d" , 1[a]);
}
```

The output for this program is:
(a) a[1]=3 1[a]=3
(b) a[1]=3 1[a]=0
(c) Error
(d) a[1]=3 1[a] =undefined

15. Consider the following program:

```
main( )
{
    char *v[] = { "abc" , "efg", "jkl" };
    char**p = v ;
    printf("%c" , *++p[0]);
    printf("%c" , (*++p)[0]);
}
```

The output for this program is:

(a) ef
(b) ae
(c) ce
(d) be

16. Consider the following program in C

```
main( )
{
    char *p;
    printf("%u" ,  sizeof(0));
    printf("%u" , sizeof(p));
    printf("%u" ,  sizeof((char*)0));
    printf("%u" ,  sizeof((float*)0));
}
```

The output for this program is if pointer is 4 byte

(a) 2 4 4 4
(b) 2 4 2 2
(c) 2 4 2 4
(d) None of the above

17. Consider the following program:

```
main( )
{
    int i =300;
    printf("%d"     (char)i);
}
```

The output for this program is

(a) 300
(b) 44

(c) 256
(d) None of the above

18. Which one of the following is false?
(a) Static object may be local to a block or external to all blocks
(b) The variable declared outside all blocks, at the same label as function definition, are always global
(c) Variable declared registers are static;
(d) Address of register variable can't be determined;

19. Consider the following statement
s1 : Evaluating the address of an object value after indirection is simply object.
s2 : Evaluating an object value from indirecting after taking its address is not the object.

Which of the following is true about s1 and s2
(a) Only s1 is correct
(b) Both s1 and s2 is correct
(c) Only s2 is correct
(d) None of s1 and s2 is correct

20. A function type declared as float f() actually return
(a) float
(b) double
(c) long double
(d) int

Answer With Detailed Explanations

Test 3

1. (a)

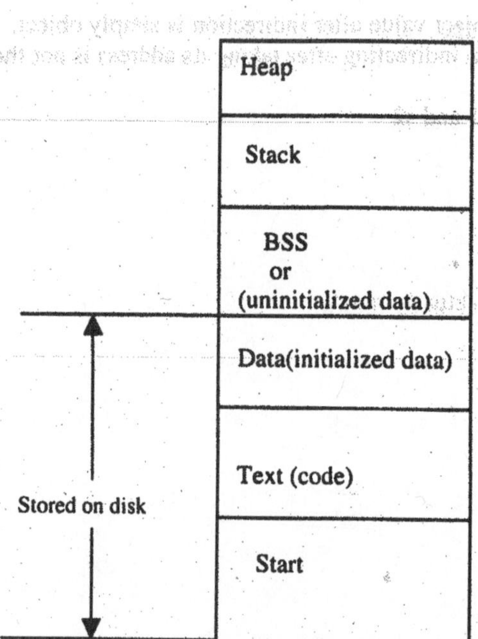

Typical subdivision of run time memory into code and data

The start segment holds information that is used by the operating system to load the program. Typically, the size of the various segments are stored there, operating system allocates a block of memory large enough to hold the remainder of the program, called the executable image. The code and data segments are the copied directly from the disk into memory. The code segments holds the executable code, the data segment holds initialized data. Hence an initialized static local variable comes up with an initial value, if value is changed it stays changed– the initial value is read from the disk into the proper place in memory. There are two types of initialized data. Variable that have given initial values and declared constants and whose values are not expected to change. The bss segment which holds all uninitialised data, is initialized to all zeros at load time. The stack pointer is initialized to point at the correct part of the stack segments that holds the run –time stack used for functions call .The heap is used, in C, by the memory –allocation subroutines malloc and free.

2. (b)

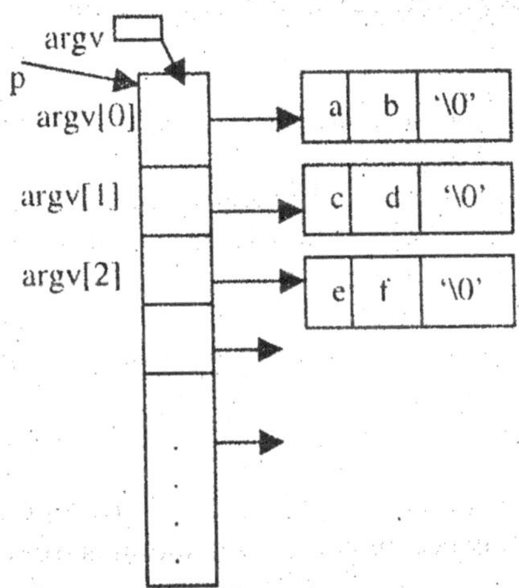

p+=sizeof(int) point to argv[2]
(p+=sizeof(int))[-1] points to argv[1]

3. (d)
See explanation 1

4. (a)
bss(block starting with symbol) contain uninitialized data
v is initialized so it does not remain in bss

5. (b)
C contain following item in stack at run time memory organization:
- Automatic variable
- Return address of function
- Function parameter

6. (b)

p: [ ] ++p->a

5	4	7	8	9	5	7	4	3	9	8	'\0'	5	6

++p->a increments a , not p, because the implied parenthesization is ++ (p->a) parentheses can be used to alter the binding.
*p->a fetches what ever a points to (4) ,*p->a++ increments a after accessing whatever it points to(7) .(*p->a)++ increments whatever a points to(first print then increment)

7. (a)
Compiler allocate memory in the stack frame for all automatic variable whether or not their scope are become active

8. (c)
++i > ++j (11 > 6) true .Then (i++) is executed first it assign value to k that is 11 then incremented and become s 12 (j++ is not executed because condition is true)

9. (a)
j is pointing to an object of integer type when increment j it point to next object of int type that is stored in stack,

10. (b)
unsigned int, obey the law of arithmetic modulo 2^n where n is the number of bits in the representation and thus arithmetic on unsigned quantities can never overflow.
(65545+65545)%65536; = 18 /* 2^{16} */

11. (c)
When we call ripple value of the first argument passed to ripple is collected in the n that is 3. va_start initialize p to point to first unnamed argument that is 5 (first argument).Each call of va_arg return an argument and step p to the next argument. va_arg uses a type name to determine what type to return and how big a step to take
Consider inner loop
(; i ; i&=i-1) k++ /* count number of 1 bit in i *
in five number of 1 bits is (101) 2
in seven number of 1 bits is (111) 3
hence k return 5

example
let i= 9 = 1001
i-1 = 1000
(i-1) +1 = i

```
 1000
   +1
 ----
 1001
```

The right most 1 bit of i has corresponding 0 bit in i-1 this way i & i-1, in a two complement number system will delete the right most 1 bit I(repeat until I become 0 gives number of 1-bits)

12. (d)
Program never terminates it print 0 1 .... 01 ..... 01 (infinite loop)
Consider expression i^j || i-- || --j
When while loop executes first times?
t1= i^j = 1^1 =0 ;
t2= i-- // first use value then increment so t2 become true
t3 =--j // t3 not evaluated because evaluation stop as soon as the truth is known
Second times on ward
t1 =i^j = 0^1=1 // remember --j is not evaluated so t1 is always true so it becomes while(1)

13. (c)

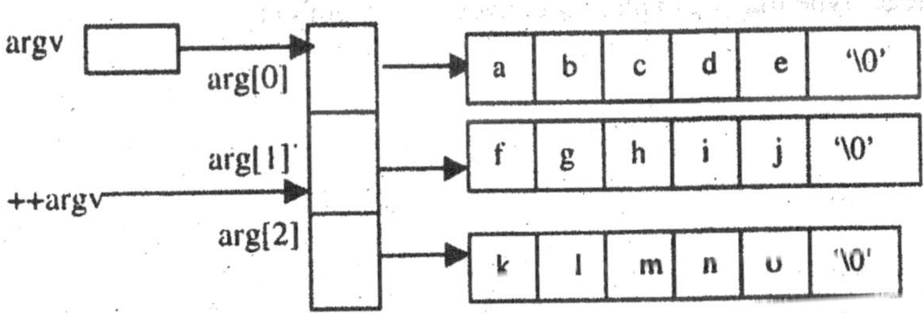

while(++argv, --argc,--i)
expression
(++argv, --argc,--i)
Results in the left-to-right evaluation of each, with the value and type of --i giving the result of the whole expression.
While executes two times first time argv point to arg[1] second times it points to arg[2]

14. (a)
The array subscript operation is defined as T1 [T2] compiler convert to it as *(T1+T2) that is equivalent to *(T2 + T1) is equivalent to T2 [T1] remember subscript operation is commutative operation.

15. (d)

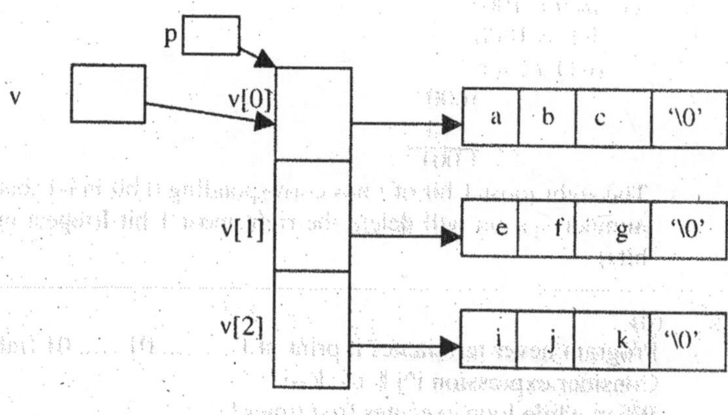

evaluate *++p[0]

[ ] has higher precedence than ++ so p[0] is evaluated first p[0] = *p contain address of "abc" ,++ increment it to point b now *p is b
(*++p) [0] , first pointer is incremented now it point to v[1] , (*++p) contain address of " efg" (*++v)[0] is e

16 (a)
An object of integer type may be explicitly converted to a pointer

17 (b)

int is 2 byte

i= 0 0 0 0 0 0 0 1 | 0 0 1 0 1 1 0 0

byte 2 byte 1

(char) i = 00101100 = 44

18. (c)
Static declaration applied to external variable or function. Variable declared outside all blocks, at the same label as function definition, are always global. registers variable can't be static; address of register variable can't be determined.

19. (b)

Consider following program

```
main( )
{
    char x[] = "abcde";
    printf("%d ,%d", x+3 , &*(x+3) )
    printf("%d ,%d", x+3 , *&(x+3))
}
```

x[i] = (*(x+i))

&x[i] = &(*(x+i))

C precedence rule evaluate & and * from right to left, so we can remove the outer parenthesis that is

&x[i] = &*(x+i)

reduced to

&x[i] = (x+i)

apply the indirection operator to a pointer offset, this evaluation to what the pointer points to if you subsequently apply the address operator, the compiler produces the pointer offset you started with the cancel each other out.

20. (b)

A function type declared as float f() actually return double

Test 4

1. Consider the following program:

```
char*concat(char*, char*);
main( )
{
   printf("%s\n" , concat("real"   "time"));
}
char*concat(char*s1, char*s2)
{
   char buf[40] ;
   return strcat(strcpy(buf,s1) ,s2 );
}
```

The output for this program is:
(a) real
(b) time
(c) real time
(d) None of the above

2. Consider following code segment

```
e 1;
while (e2 )
{
   stmt;
   e3;
}
```

Equivalent for statement is
(a) for (el; e2 ;e3)
 stmt;
(b) for (el; e3 ;e2)
 stmt;
(c) for (el; e2 ;e3) ;
 stmt;
(d) for (e3; e2 ;el)
 stmt ;

3. Consider the following program:

```
main(  )
```

```
{
    double buf[80];
    double  *s, *r;
    r  = buf ;
    s = r + 5;
    printf("%d" , s-r);
}
```

The output for this program is:

(a) Pointer subtraction is not allowed
(b) 5
(c) 40
(d) 20

4. Consider the following program:

```
void process (char**);
main(  )
{
    static char  *table[] = {
        "satyam : truth =t " ,
        "shivam : shiv =s" ,
        "sundaram: beauty =b",
        (char*)0
    };
    int j;
    process (table);
    for (j =0 ; table[j] ; j++)
    printf("%s\n" , table[j]);
}
void process (char ** table)
{
    char *p;
    while( p =*table++) {
    while(*p++ !='·' ) ;
    *p ='\0';
    }
}
```

(a) satyam :
shivam :
sundaram:

(b) truth
shiv
beauty

(c) satyam : truth =t
shivam : shiv =s
sundaram: beauty =b

(d) none

5 Consider following declaration

```
main( )
{
    int count;
    printf("12345 %n6" , &count);
    printf("count=%d" , count);
}
```

The output for this program is:

(a) 123456
count =5

(b) 12345%n6
count =5

(c) 12345
count = l

(d) 123456
count = l

6. Consider the following program:

```
main( )
{
    static int a[2][3] = { { 1,2,3}, {4,5,6} };
    printf("%d" , a[1,1][1,2]);
}
```

The output for this program is:

(a) 8
(b) 3
(c) 6
(d) Error

7. Consider the following program:

```
main( )
{
```

```
    char *p = " real time" ;
    printf(":% .*s:\n" , 5 ,p);
    printf(":%12.*s:" , 10 , p);
}
```

The output for this program is:

(a) : real:
: real time:

(b) : real time:
: real time:]

(c) : real time:
: real:

(e) None of the above

8. Consider the following program:

```
void string(char*) ;
main( )
{
    char *p = " tit for tat";
    string(p);
    printf("%s" , p);
}
void string( char *q)
{
    char * r = q + strlen(q) -1 ;

    for ( ; q< r ; q ++ , r--) {
        *q =  *q ^*r ;
        *r  =  *r^*q ;
        *q  =  *q^*r ;
    }
}
```

(a) tit for tat ;
(b) tat rof tit;
(c) tat for tit
(d) None of the above

9. Select the correct declaration for following statement
Array of 3 pointer to function that return pointer to char

(a) char (*tmp[3]) ()
(b) char * (* buf[3]) ()
(c) char * buf[3] ()

(d) char * (buf [3]) []

10. For write a function that process a variable-length argument which of the following macro is used?

(a) va_end
(b) va_start
(c) va_arg
(d) All of the above

11. Consider following statement(keyword)

goto	(1)
continue	(2)
break	(3)
return	(4)

which of the following is/are jump statement?

(a) only 1and 2
(b) only 3 and 4
(c) only 1and 3
(d) All are jump statement

12. Consider the following expression

*p--	(1)
*--p	(2)
--*p	(3)
(*p)--	(4)

Which of the following is a lvalue?

(a) 3 and 4 only
(b) 1 and 2 only
(c) 1 and 3 only
(d) 1 and 4 only

13. Consider the following program:

```
/* try.c*/
main( int argc , char * argv[])
{
   if( argc ==1) {
   printf("error");
   exit(1);
   }
   while(**argv , --argc) {
   printf("%s" , *++argv);
   while(argc , **argv) {
```

```
    printf("%c" , *(*argv)++);
    }
    putcha('\n')
    }
}
```

The output for this program is If input is $ try sun run

(a) sun : sun
    run : run

(b) sun : sun
    run : run

(c) sun :
    run :

(d) run : run|

Consider the following program:

```
main( )
{
    struct a{
        int tmp[3] ;
    };
    int j;
    static int p[3] = {  1,2,3};
    static int q[3] = {  4,5,6};
    *(struct a*)q=*(struct a *)p;
    for( j = 0 ; j <3 ;  j++)
    printf(" %3d" ,  *(q+j));
}
```

The output for this program is

(a) 1 5 6

(b) 4 5 6

(c) 1 2 3

(d) None of the above

15. Consider the following program:

```
#pragma inline
static int try ( int x1 , int x2)
{
    asm mov AX, x1
    asm sub AX, x2
    return  _AX ;
```

```
}
main(int argc , char *argv[])
{
    register  int p ;
    register int q;
    int result   ;
    if(argc !=3)
    printf("error");
    p = atoi(argv[1]);
    q= atoi(argv[2]);
    result try(p , q);
    printf(" result = %d" , result ) ;
}
```

The output for this program is if input is test 800 300

(a) 500
(b) 800
(c) can not return register from function
(d) 0

16. Which of the following is false?
(a) Static object can not be local to a block
(b) Object may be made local to a particular source file by use of the static key word
(c) Objects may be made global to an entire program by using key word extern
(d) The object declared outside all blocks, at the same level as function definition, are always global.

17. Which of the following is false?
(a) A structure may not contain a member of incomplete type
(b) It is possible to declare a structure or union containing an instance to itself
(c) A structure or union may contain a pointer to an instance of itself
(d) A structure or union specifier with a list but no tag creates a unique type

18. Non local jump (from one function to another function) can be done using
(a) Setjmp
(b) Longjmp
(c) Goto
(d) both (a) and (b)

19. Which of the following declaration is incomplete type?

struct tag; (1)
struct tag { int a }; (2)
typedef struct { int a: } abc (3)

(a) 1and 2 only
(b) 2 and 3 only

(c) I and 3 only
(d) I only

20. Consider the following program:

```
typedef union  {
   struct {
      int a ;
   } A ;
   struct     {
      int  a ;
      float b;
   }B;
}dd;
main( )
{
   dd D;

   D.A.a=3;
   D.B.b=5.3;
   printf( " %d " , D.B.a );
}
```

The output for this program is
(a) 3
(b) 0
(c) 5.3
(d) None of the above

Answer With Detailed Explanations

Test 4

1. (d)
Since buf has automatic storage, it lives on the stack, when we return from concat, the stack frames disappears. This means the memory used for the old stack frames will be reclaimed. It is possible that program may work but this is unlikely. Never return the address of an automatic variable from a function.

2. (a)

```
e1;
while (e2 )
{
    statement;
    e3;
}
```

is equivalent to

```
for (e1; e2 ;e3)
    stmt ;
```

3. (b)
Arithmetic operator (-) with pointer is allowed if s and r points to object of the same type T the expression s-r, r-s gives the number of objects between the two pointer. Depending on the implementation result is an int or long .Its sign may be negative, depends on which address in memory (s, or r) is greater.

4. (a)

5. (a)
n writes the number of characters written so far by this call to printf is written into the count .

6. (c)
Comma operator discard the first number it's become as a [1][2]

7. (a)
A width or precision may be specified as * in which case the value is computed by the next argument (which must be an int).

8. (b)
Program reverse character in string using EX-OR operator

9. (b)
A C declaration may include various combinations of pointers, array and functions. To decipher a declaration the compiler has sort out the attribute listed below.

Attribute	Meaning
( )	function
[]	array
*	pointer

() and [] have higher precedence then * and evaluate from left to right
To decipher a declaration substitute English keyword where an attribute appears
English keyword for declaration attribute

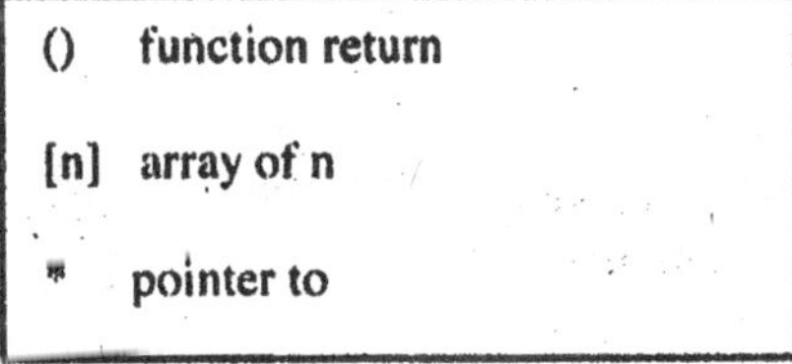

()	function return
[n]	array of n
*	pointer to

Start from right to left to decipher declaration
- Start with the identifier
- See right for an attribute
- If attribute found Substitute English key word
  Else see to the left
- Continue Right to left rule
- Stop when reach data type

Example

attribute (pointer to) identifier attribute(array)

Unsigned int r

Now declaration become r is array of 2 pointer to unsigned type
Consider declaration char * (* buf[5]) ()
buf is identifier see right we find buf is an array see left we see it is an array of pointers, see right we find array element is an address of a function that return pointer to char
buf is an array of 3 pointers to function that return pointer to char.

10. (d)
The header<stdarg.h> provides following macro for stepping a list of function argument of unknown number and type
va_start(va_list va, finalarg);
va_arg (va_list va, type);
void va_end(va_list va);

11. (d)
A continue statement appear only within an iterative statement. It causes control to pass to the loop continuation portion of the smallest enclosing statement

```
while (...)     // loop 1
   {
   ......
   while(... )  //loop2
      {
      .......
      continue ; // only continue loop 2

      }
   }
```

break statement appear only in an iteration statement or a switch statement, and terminates execution of the smallest enclosing such statement

```
while (1)     // loop 1
   {
   int i =3;
   ......
   while(1 )  //loop2
      {
      .......
      if(i==3)
      break; ; // only break loop 2 and  program is in infinite
         loop

      }
   }
```

A function returns to its caller by the return statement.
Goto is a jump statement within same function

12. (b)
A lvalue is usually an expression/object that appears on the left side of an assignment statement. Something that appears on the right side of an assignment statement (appropriately called an rvalue) .lvalue must have storage associated with it or compilers treat the following as lvalues.

- Variable names with data type, float , int, double , etc. also pointers, structures, union, and array elements
- Result from applying the indirection operator (*)
- The result from applying the structure member operator or the structure pointer perator -> if the member is also an lvalue

lvalue operator are

C compiler treats following as rvalues

- constants
- function name
- enumerated values
- array name

Name of an array is a constant (rvalue), ++ , -- operator can not be applied to the name of an array
Example a-- , --a is not allowed

```
*p -= 3;
*--p =5`;
```

both expression are lvalues

```
--*p = 3;
(*p)-- = 5;
```

Both expressions are illegal and produce compilation errors. Both expression applying the -- operator to object (an int) instead of the pointers.

13. (a)
Program has two while loops. First while loop (while(**argv , --argc)) ignore first argument) becomes (--argc) and it executes over the number of command line argument argc. *++argv increment argv before it display the argument with *argv. Second while loop (while(argc , *argv) ignore first argument evaluate only * argv so it become while(*argv)

14. (c)
Array p contain 3 number and array q hold 3 numbers

Statement (struct a*) q = (struct a*) p moves 3 integer p to q

15. (a)

The asm statement allows you to place assembly language statements in the middle of your C source code.

```
asm <opcode> <operands> <; or newline>
```

Any C symbols are replaced by the appropriate assembly language equivalents.

```
#pragma (directive)
```

With the #pragma directive, you can use implementation-specific directives of the form:

```
#pragma <directive_name>
```

If the compiler doesn't recognize <directive_name>, it ignores the #pragma directive without an error or warning message.

Borland C supports : #pragma inline

This tells the compiler that the source text contains inline asm statements.

16. (a)

Static object can be local to a block

17. (b)

```
struct abc { } ; /*incomplete type*/
```

if a specifier with a tag list without a list appears , an incomplete type is specified

Object with an incomplete structure or union type may be mentioned in context where there size is not needed for example in declaration not definition, for specifying a pointer, or for creating a typedef , but not otherwise.

```
size ptr ;        /* pointer to incomplete type is allowed */
struct tag {
   struct a ; /* Not possible because incomplete type*/
};
struct tag {
   struct tag ptr;  /* pointer to incomplete type is allowed*/
};
```

18. (d)

See explanation (test 1 1.)

19. (d)

If a specifier with a tag but without a list appears then an incomlete type is specified.

20. (a)

In a union that contains several structures and share a common initial sequence and if the union currently contains one of these structures, it is permitted to refer to the common initial part of any of the contained structure.

Test 5

1. Consider the following code:

```
typedef union {
   unsigned int word;
   unsigned char test[2];
}test ;
test  p = { 576 };
```

What value will p.test[0] and p.test[1] have ?
(a) 2,64
(b) 64, 2
(c) 64, 1
(d) None of the above.

2. Consider the following program:

```
int fun (int a, int b, int c)
{
   if((a>=b) &&(c<b)) return b;
   else if (a>=b) return fun(a,c,b);
   else return fun(b,a, c);
}
main( )
{
   printf("%d", try(1,2,3));

}
```

The output for this program is:
(a) 1
(b) 2
(c) 3
(d) None of the above

3. Consider following macro
__LINE__ (1)
__TIME__ (2)
__FILE__ (3)
__DATE__ (4)
__STDC__ (5)
Which of the following is true?

(a) Only 1 and 2 is predefined macro in C
(b) Only (2) and (3) is predefined macro in C
(c) All is predefined macro in C
(d) Only 4 and 5 is predefined macro in C

4. Which operator is/are really overloaded in C?
(a) * and &
(b) && and ||
(c) ++ --
(d) None of the above

5. Consider the following program:

```
main( )
{
    printf("%d" , printf("abc"));
}
```

The output for this program is:
(a) 3
(b) abc
(c) abc3
(d) None of the above

6. Consider the following program:

```
main( )
{
    printf( "%d" , sizeof( 3.5,3)) ;
}
```

(a) float
(b) double
(c) long double
(d) int

7. The following C declaration

```
struct node {
    int  i ;
    float  j ;
};
struct node *const a[3];
```

Define to be
(a) An array, of three read only pointer to a structure of type node
(b) A structure of 2 fields, each field being a pointer to an array of 10 elements
(c) A structure of three field an integer, a float, and an array of 10 elements
(d) An array, each element of which is a structure of type node

8. Consider the following C declaration

```
struct {
    short s[5];
    union {
        float y;
        long z;
    } u;
}t;
```

Assume that object of the type short, float and long occupy 2 bytes, 4 bytes, and 8 bytes respectively, the memory required for variable t ignoring alignment consideration is
(a) 22 bytes
(b) 14 bytes
(c) 18 bytes
(d) 10 bytes

9. Consider the following program:

```
int counter (int i)
{
    static int count =0;
    count - count +i ;
    return (count );
}
main( )
{
    int i , j;

    for (i=0 ; i <=5 ; i++)
    j = counter(i);
}
```

The value of j at the end of the execution of the this program is:
(a) 10
(b) 15
(c) 6
(d) 7

10. The following C declaration

```
int const * const ptr ;
```

define to be
(a) ptr is a pointer to read only int
(b) ptr is a const pointer to int
(c) ptr is a read only pointer pointer to const int
(d) None of the above

11. To arrange the n number stored in an array such that positive values occur before all negative values. Minimum number of exchange in worst case is
(a) n-1
(b) n/2
(c) n+1
(d) n

12. Consider the following code

```
int i=3;
int j=i++ + ++i;
```

What is the value of j?
(a) 4
(b) 7
(c) 8
(d) The value is implementation dependent because it is not defined in Standard C.

13. Automatic variable (except static) in C is stored in
(a) Stack section
(b) Code section
(c) Data section
(d) Heap section

14. How does the compiler process string literals?
(a) They are allocated on the stack.
(b) They are treated identically to all other arrays in every respect.
(c) Depending upon the compiler they may be allocated in a data area or code area that may be read-only.
(d) (d) None of the above

15. Consider the following program:

```
main( )
{
    int n;
    printf("%d" , f(5));
```

```
}
int f(int n)
{
    int x;
    if (n ==0)   x =0;
    else x = n +f(n-1);
    return x;
}
```

The output for this program is:
(a) 10
(b) 15
(c) 0
(d) None of the above

16. Consider the following program:

```
main( )
{
    int i ,j ;
    i =1;
    j =5;
    for(; ++i< --j ; ) continue ;
    printf ("%d  %d " , i , j);
}
```

The output for this program is:
(a) 3 4
(b) 2 4
(c) 3 2
(d) 3 3

17. If memory for run time stack is only 300 word, how big n be in factorial (n) before encountering stack overflow?
(a) 75
(b) 150
(c) 100
(d) 300

8. Consider the following code

```
char *ptr[3] = {
    "the",
    "hello",
```

```
    "word"
};
```

Correct code to print hello of the above code is:
(a) printf("%s", *(ptr+1]);
(b) printf("%s", *ptr[0]);
(c) printf("%s", *ptr[1]);
(d) printf("%s", ptr[0]);

19. Consider the following program

```
main( )
{
    float va = 3/2.0 + 1/2;
    printf("va=%.3f\n", va);
}
```

The output for this program is:
(a) va=1.500
(b) va=2.000
(c) va=0.500
(d) None of the above

20. Consider the following declaration
`int arr[5][6][7];`
the type of arr[0]?
(a) Pointer to array [5] of int
(b) Array [6] of array [7] of int
(c) Pointer to array [6] of array [7] of int
(d) Array [7] of array [6] of int

Answer With Detailed Explanations

Test 5

1. (b)
where the least –significant byte is stored at the lowest address

$(576)_{10} = (0000001001000000)_2 = (00000010 \quad 01000000)$

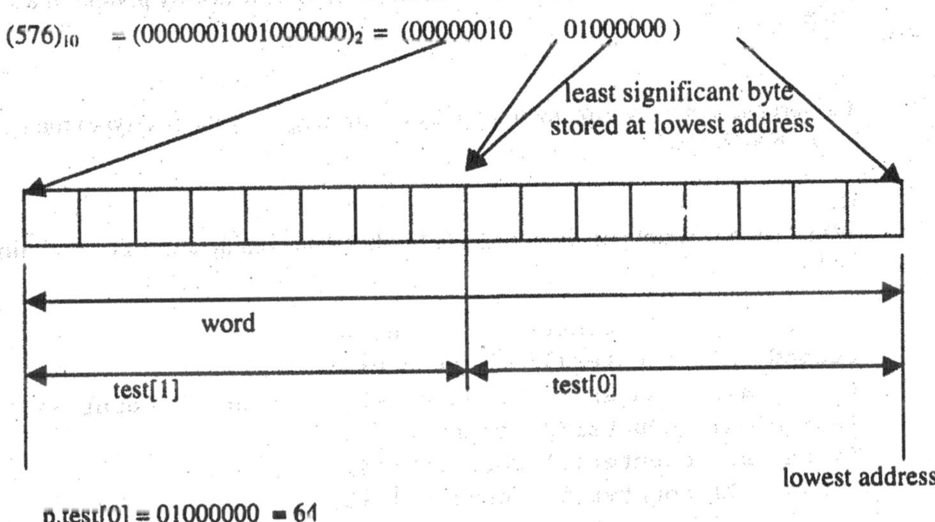

p.test[0] = 01000000 = 64
p.test[1]= 00000010 = 2

2. (b)
find middle (2) element

3. (c)

4. (a)
* is used as indirection operator as well as multiplication operator

```
int x ;
int *ptr= &x;
*ptr = 10;
x*x
& is used bitwise and operator and  address operator
if(2&3) then printf(" true");
int x
```

```
int *ptr = &x;
```

5. (c)
printf return the number of bytes output, in this case printf return 3

6. (d)
A pair of expression separated by comma is evaluated left –to right, and the value of the left expression is discarded. The type and value of the result are the type and value of the right expression

7. (a)
struct node *const a[3] defined to be an array, of three read only pointer to a structure of type node

8. (c)
the variable u will occupy memory 8 bytes(the largest of the two type) total memory is 5*2 +8 = 18 bytes

9. (b)
Static variable count remain in existence rather than coming and going each time function is called

```
so  first call counter(0)  count =0
second call counter(1) count = 0+1;
third call counter(2) count = 1+2; /* count = count +i */
fourth call counter(3) count = 3+3;
fifth call counter(4) count = 6+4;
sixth call counter(5) count = 10+5;
```

10. (c)
int const *const ptr: defined to be read only pointer to const int :
Note : declarations: int const p; and const int p; are identical

11. (b)
Minimum no of exchange require in the worst case would be n/2 as the worst case would be one where all the negative number occurs before the positive numbers

12. (d)
The value is implementation dependent because it is not defined in Standard C

13. (a)
Automatic variable in C is stored in stack

14. (c)

Depending upon the compiler they may be allocated in a data area or code area that may be read-only.

15. (b)

if(n!=0) x = 5 + f(5 –1) ⟶ (4 +f(4-1) ⟶ (3 +f(3-1) ⟶ (2+f(2-1) ⟶ (1 +f(0) ⟶ 0

x = 5+10 ⟵ .... ⟵ ⟵

16. (d)
when i =3 and j is =3 condition is false and loop terminate

17. (c)
```
floor(300/3)   /* old value   new value   operator */
```

18. (a)
```
ptr[1]   or *(ptr+1)
```

19. (a)
1/2 becomes =0 integer division

20. (b)
```
Array [6] of array [7] of int
```
The type of a variable of incomplete array type is completed by another, complete, declaration for the variable for example

```
int arr[5][6][7] declare  a three-dimensional array of integers.
arr[0] is array [6] of array [7] of int
arr[j] and arr[j][k] /* type " array" */
arr[j][k][[l] /*type int */
```

Test 6

1. Consider the following code: .

```
f ( unsigned int x   , unsigned int y)
{
   while(x!=y)  {
      if(x>y)  x = x-y ;
      else      y= y-x ;
   }
   printf("%d" , x);
}
```

What does the above code do?

(a) Compute the GCD of two numbers
(b) Divide the largest number by the smallest number
(c) Compute the LCM of two numbers
(d) None of the above

Consider the following program:

```
main( )
{
   unsigned char c;
   int i;
   c = 128;
   i=0;
   while (i<8){
   test(&c);
   ++i;
   }
   printf("%d" , c) ;
}
void test(unsigned char *c)
{
   union {
      unsigned u;
      unsigned char c[2];
   } uvar = {0};
   uvar.c[0] = *c;
   uvar.u = uvar.u << 1;
   if(uvar.c[1]) uvar.c[0] = uvar.c[0] | 1;
```

```
    *c = uvar.c[0];
}
```

The output for this program is:
(a) 1
(b) 64
(c) 128
(d) 256

3. Which of the following is a true statement about a rvalue?
(a) A rvalue is, the value appearing on the left side of an assignment statement.
(b) A rvalue is an expression referring to an object
(c) A rvalue is, the value appearing on the right side of an assignment and can not appear left side such as(a+b)
(d) None of the above

4. Consider the following program:

```
main( )
{
    float  a[3];
    printf("%d" , sizeof(a));
    printf("%d", sizeof(&a));
}
```

The output for this program is:
(a) 12 4
(b) 3 2
(c) 12 2
(d) None of the above

5. Which one of the following is a true statement about an wchar_t ?
(a) Purpose of wchar_t is to accommodate extended set of characters that can not be represented in the char type .
(b) wchar_t is a char type defined in standard header <stdio.h>
(c) wcar_t is a float type defined in standard header <stddef.h>
(d) None of the above

6. Consider the following program:

```
??=include<stdio.h>
??=include<string.h>
main( )
??<
    int a??(21??) ;
```

```
    int i =3 ;
    if( i??'i)
    strcpy(a , "tri??/n graph" );
    else strcpy(a ,"ansi??/nc") ;
    printf("%s " , a ) ;
??>
```

The output for this program is:

(a) tri
graph

(b) ansi
c

(c) Not compile

(d) ansi c

7. Consider the following program:

```
main( )
{
    char *p ;
    char *line[] = { "sunday" , "monday" ,"tuesday" };
    if( p = strstr(line[0], "day" ))
    printf("%s" , p);
}
```

The output for this program is:

(a) sun

(b) day

(c) Sunday

(d) None of the above

8. Consider the following program:

```
main( )
{
    char *p ;
    char *line[] = {  "monday" ,"tuesday" };
    if( p = strchr(line[0], 'd' ))
    printf("%s" , p);
}
```

The output for this program is:

(a) day

(b) ay

(c) Monday
(d) None of the above

9. Consider the following program:

```
main( )
{
   char *p ;
   char *line[] = {  "moonmoon" ,"tuesday" };
   if( p = strrchr(line[0], 'o' ))
   printf("%s" , p);
}
```

The output for this program is:
(a) onmoon
(b) oonmoon
(c) on
(d) None of the above

10. Consider the following program:

```
main( )
{
   char *ptr;
   ptr = strtok("jan,feb,mar", ",");
   printf(ptr);
   do {
      ptr = strtok('\0', ",");
      if(ptr) printf("%5s", ptr);
   } while(ptr);
   return 0;
}
```

The output for this program is:
(a) jan feb mar
(b) jan,feb,mar
(c) janfebmar
(d) None of the above

11. If following program finds the prime numbers from 2 to 100.

```
main( )
{
   int i, j, prime;
   for(i=2; i<100; i++) {
```

```
        prime = 1;
        for(j=2; j <= i/2; j++)
                 s1
        if(prime) printf("%d is prime.\n", i);
        }
}
```

s1 should be

(a) if(i%j) prime=0;
(b) if(!(i%j)) prime=0;
(c) if(!(i/j)) prime=0;
(d) if((i/j)) prime=0;

Consider the following program:

```
main( )
{
    int i ;
    char *p ="2" ;
    char table[][2][10] = {
       {"1", " one"},
       {"2", "two"},
       {"", ""}
    };
    i = 0;
    while(strcmp(table[i][0], "" )) {
    if(!strcmp(p, table[i][0])) {
    printf("%s", table[i][1]);
    break;
    }
    i++;
    }
    if(!strcmp(table[i][0], ""))
    printf("in table\n");
}
```

The output for this program is:

(a) two
(b) in table
(c) one
(d) None of the above

13. Consider the following program:

```
main( )
{
   union t_type {
      int  in ;
      long lon;
   } u= {65};
   printf("%ld", u.lon);
}
```

The output for this program is:
(a) 0
(b) undefined
(c) 65
(d) Not compile because union can not be initialized

14. Consider the following program:

```
main( )
{
   unsigned int i =2;

   i = ((((i<<6)-1)^127)   ;
   printf("%u" , i );
}
```

The output for this program is:
(a) 127
(b) 1
(c) 0
(d) None of the above

5. Which one of the following is a true statement about an lvalue?
(a) An lvalue is, the value appearing on the right side of an assignment statement.
(b) An lvalue is an expression referring to an object
(c) An lvalue is the result of an arithmetic operation such as(a+b) is an lvalue.
(d) None of the above

6. Consider the following program:

```
main( )
{
   unsigned char c;
   c = 65;
```

```
    bin(c);
}
void bin(unsigned i)
{
    unsigned n=2;
    for(n=n<<6; n>0; n=n/2)
    if(i & n) printf("1 ");
    else printf("0 ");
}
```

The output for this program is:

(a) 0 1 0 0 0 0 0 1
(b) 0 0 0 0 0 0 0 0
(c) 1 1 1 1 1 1 1 1
(d) None of the above

17. Consider the following program:

```
main( )
{
    #line 5 "try.c"
    printf("%s ,  %d",        __FILE__ ,  __LINE__ );
}
```

The output for this program is:

(a) try.c , 6
(b) try.c , 5
(c) try.c , 1
(d) None of the above

18. calloc(m,n) is eqivalent to

(a) p = malloc(m*n) ; memset(p , 1 ,n) ;
(b) p = malloc(m*n) ; memset(p , 0 m*n) ;
(c) p = malloc(m*n) ; memset(p , 0 m) ;
(e) p= malloc(m) ; memset(p , 0 m*n) ;

19. Consider the following statement
s1 : The scope of a name defined with #define is file
s2 : The scope of a name defined with typedef is file
Which of the following is true

(a) s1 and s2 is correct
(b) s1 is correct s2 is incorrect
(c) s1 is incorrect s2 is correct
(d) s1 nad s2 is incorrect

20. Consider the following program:

```
main( )
{
   unsigned int i=0x53;
   unsigned int j=0x12;
   unsigned int sub;
   _asm {
      mov          eax,i;  move i into eax register
      sub          eax,j; subtract j from eax
      mov          sub,eax      ;store eax in sub
   }
   printf("%x", sub);
}
```

The output for this program is:

(a) 64
(b) 41
(c) 32
(d) 66

Answer With Detailed Explanations

Test 6

1. (a)
Function compute GCD of two number

2. (c)

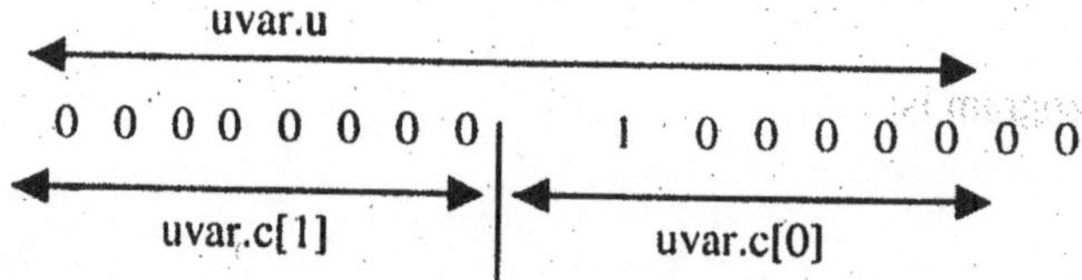

Only uvar.c[0] is rotated to 8 times it again becomes 1 0 0 0 0 0 0 0

3. (c)
The expression
a + b
is not an lvalue: a + b = 5 is illegal because the expression on the left is not related to an object.
Such expressions are often called rvalues

4. (c)
Remember the difference between a and &a
&a has type pointer to array of 3 floats or float (*a) [3] so sizeof(&a) is sizeof pointer that is 2 ,sizeof (a) is 12 /* float is 4 byte */

5. (a)
wchar_t is an integer type defined in the standard header<stddef.h> and used for the extended set of characters that can not be representsd in the char type .

6. (b)
Trigraph sequence are new with the ANSI C standard. All occurrence of the following trigraph are replaced by corresponding single character. Replacements occurs before any other processing

TRIGRAPH SEQUENCE	REPLACED BY
??=	#
??/	\
??'	^
??(	[
??)	]
??!	|
??<	{
??>	}
??-	~

7. (b)
The standard library function char *strstr(const char* p, const char*q) returns pointer to first occurrence of string q in p or NULL if not present strstr(line[0] , "day") return pointer to "day"

8. (a)
The standard library function char* strchr(const char* p, char p) returns pointer to first occurrence of q in p or NULL if not present strstr(line[0] , 'd') return pointer to "day"

9. (c)
The standard library function char* strrchr(const char* **p,** char p) returns pointer to last occurrence of q in p or NULL if not present strrstr(line[0] , 'o') return pointer to "on"

10. (a)
The standard library function char* strtok(char* p, const char* q) search p for token delimited by characters from q

11. (b)
if (i%j) remainder is zero then i is divided by j hence can not be prime

12. (a)
This program is a lookup program in table, 2 is in table hence it print two

13. (c)

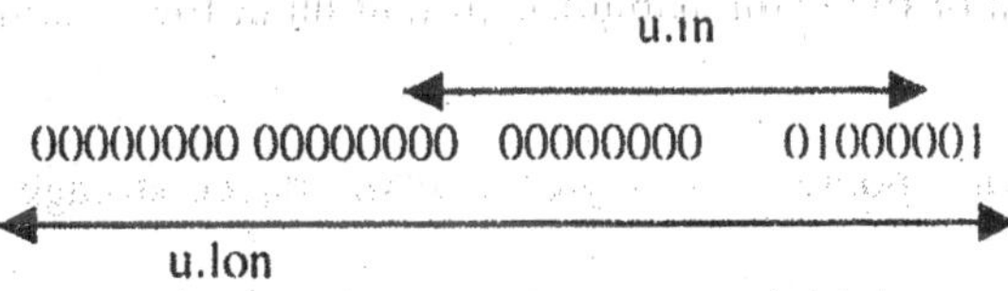

14. (c)
i<<6 is eqivalent to multiplication by 2^6 (2* 2^6 becomes 128 – 1 = 127 , 127^127 = 0)

15. (b)
An lvalue is an object locator, an expression that designates an object. An example of an lvalue expression is *ptr, where ptr is any expression evaluating to a non-null pointer. Historically, the l stood for "left," meaning that an lvalue could legally stand on the left of an assignment statement. Now, only modifiable lvalues can legally stand on the left of an assignment

16. (a)
program print binary representation of 65
n=n<<6 becomes = 128

```
    1 0 0  0 0 0 0 0
&   0 1 0  0 0 0 0 1
-------------------
    0 0 0  0 0 0 0 0
```

So if condition become false print 1
n=n/2 is equivalent to (n=n>>2) so next times n becomes n =0 1 0 0 0 0 0 0 and condition is tested (i&n). it becomes true and print 1.Similarly loop executed until n becomes zero

17. (a)
#line 5 "try.c" this causes compiler to consider that line number of the next source line is given by the 5
__LINE__ contain the current source line number (that is 6)
consider the following program. This program print 8

```
main(void)
{
    #line 5 "try.c"
    int i; /* line 6 */
    int j; /*  line 7 */
    printf("%s ,  %d",     __FILE__ ,   __LINE__ ); /* line 8 */
}
```

current input file is named as try.c
__FILE__ contain the name of file being compiled current input file is named as try.c

18. (b)
void malloc(size_t n) return a pointer to n bytes of uninitialized storage , or NULL if the request can not be satisfied
void calloc(size_t n , size_t m) return a pointer to enough space for an array of n object of the specified size , or NULL if the request can not be satisfied . The storage is initialized to zero.

19. (b)
The scope of a name defined with #define is file
Example

```
f(  )
{
   #define  i =75
}
main( )
{
   printf( "%d" , i)  /* no error */
}
f(  )
{
   typedef int  i ; / *local scope */
}
main( )
{
printf( "%d" , i)  /* error */
}
```

20. (b)
%x is used for hexadecimal ($41_{16} = 65_{10}$)
Note : program is compiled using Microsoft visual c++ 6.0
`_asm (keyword)`
The _asm statement allows you to place assembly language statements in the middle of your C source code.
`asm <opcode> <operands> <; or newline>`
Any C symbols are replaced by the appropriate assembly language equivalents. If you want to include a number of _asm statements, surround them with braces:

```
_asm {

}
```

Test 7

1. Consider the following code segment in C

```
unsigned int  i ;
i= 36751       /*  binary representation of 36751 is  10001111
10001111    */
```

Correct expression to set bit 8 to 0 is (as 10001111 00001111) given by:

(a) i &= ~(lu <<7);
(b) i &= (lu << 7);
(c) i |= ~(lu <<7);
(d) i ^= ~(lu << 7)

2. Consider the following program:

```
main( )
{
   struct test {
      int  i;
      char  c ;
      union {
         int iu ;
         char cu ;
      }u ;
   };
   struct test  su = {0};
   printf("%d %d %d %d" ,su.u.cu, su.u.iu, su.c , su.i);
}
```

The output for this program is:

(a) 0 0 undefined undefined
(b) 0 0 0 0
(c) 0 undefined undefined undefined
(d) Undefined undefined undefined undefined

3. To make cetrtain that the contents of a file std.h are included only once , the contents of the file are surrounded with

(a) # ifndef(STD)
#defined STD
#endf

(b) # ifdef(STD)
#defined STD
#endf

(c) # if !defined(STD)
#defined STD
#endf

(d) Both (a) and (c)

4. Consider the following program:

```
void execute (int [] , int , int);
main( )
{
   static int a[] = {5, 3,4,2,1,6,8} ;
   int temp ;
   int p,s,e,i ;
   s =0 ;
   p =s;
   e =sizeof(a)/sizeof(a[0]) ;
   for ( i = s +1 ; i<e ; i++)
      if(a[i] < a[s])
      execute(a , ++p ,i);
   execute(a , s ,p);
   for (i=0; i< e ; i++)
   printf("%d " , a[i]);
}
void execute( int a[] , int i , int j)
{
   int temp ;
   temp = a[i];
   a[i] =a[j];
   a[j] = temp ;
}
```

The output for this program is:

(a) 5 3 4 2 1 6 8

(b) 8 3 4 2 1 6 5

(c) 1 3 4 2 5 6 8

(d) 8 6 1 2 4 3 5

5. Consider the following program:

```
void tmp(char *);
main( )
{
   char *p = "abcdef" ;
   tmp(p) ;
```

```
}
void tmp( char *s)
{
    char *q = ++s;
    while( *q) ++q;
    printf("%d" , q-s);
}
```

The output for this program is:
(a) 6
(b) 5
(c) 3
(d) Programs not compile

6. Consider the following program:

```
void tmp(char *);
main( )
{
    char *p = "abcdef" ;
    tmp(p) ;
}
void tmp( char *s)
{
    char *q = &s[6];
    char *p= &s[6];
    ++p;
    printf("%d %d" , p-q);
    ++p;
    printf("%d" , p-q);
}
```

The output for this program is:
(a) undefined undefined
(b) 1 2
(c) 1 undefined
(d) None of the above

7. Consider the following program:

```
int x=3;
int y =5;
main( )
{
```

```
    int x =x;
    static y;
    y=y;
    printf("%d %d" , x, y) ;
}
```

The output for this program is:
(a) undefined undefined
(b) undefined 0
(c) 3 5
(d) 0 0

8. Consider the following program:

```
main( )
{
    while(1) {
        int i =0;
        while(i<10) {
            ++i;
            for( ;;) {
                if(++i <5)
                continue;
                break;
            }
        }
    printf("%d" ,i);
    break; ;
    }
}
```

The output for this program is:
(a) 10
(b) 11
(c) 9
(d) Program not terminate

9. Consider the following program:

```
main( )
{
    int sum ;
    enum  tmp { A , B, C=5, D, E} ;
    sum = A+B+C+D+E ;
```

```
    printf("%d" , sum) ;
}
```

The output for this program is:
(a) 20
(b) 19
(c) 15
(d) None of the above

10. Consider following statement
s1: Different enumeration may have same name
s2: Values must be distinct in the same enumeration
Which of the following is true?
(a) s1 and s2 are correct
(b) only s1 is correct
(c) only s2 is correct
(d) s1 and s2 is incorrect

11. Consider the following program:

```
main( )
{
    int a =2;
    if(++a^++a && (a^a)||++a)
    printf("%d" , a);
}
```

The output for this program is:
(a) 4
(b) 5
(c) 6
(d) 3

12. Consider the following program:

```
main( )
{
    unsigned int a =2;
    unsigned int b =3;
    unsigned int c =5 ;
    a <<=c>b>a ^a<c<b ;
    printf("%u" , a) ;
}
```

The output for this program is:
(a) 8
(b) 4
(c) 2
(d) None of the above

13. Consider the following code segment in C
unsigned int i =521 ; / binary representation of i is 00000010 00001001
Correct expression to invert only 2 bits that begins at position 3 is

position 3

(exp 0000001000001001 becomes 0 0 0 0 0 0 1 0 0 0 0 0 0 0 1 0 1)

(a) i = i ^((~ (~(i^i)<<2))<<2) ;
(b) i= i^((~(~1<< 2))<< 2)
(c) i = i ^((~ (~(0^1)<<2))<<2) ;
(d) None of the above

14. Consider the following program:

```
main( )
{
   unsigned int j,i ;
   union {
      unsigned int i;
      unsigned char a[2] ;
   }u ={129};
   int n ;
   n=1;
   while(n-->0) {
      j =((u.a[0]&1) <<7);
      u.a[0] = u.a[0]>>1;
      u.a[0]= u.a[0] |j ;
   }
   printf("%d" , u.i) ;
}
```

The output for this program is:
(a) 1
(b) 192
(c) 64
(d) 128

15. Consider the following program:

```
main( )
{
    int i =5 ;
    switch(i) {
    static int i;
    i =3;
    i= i*i ;
    case 3 :
        i =i+i;
    case 4 :
        i =i+i ;
    case 5 :
        i = i+i ;
    default :
        i = i+i ;
    printf("%d" , i) ;
    }
    printf("%d" , i) ;
}
```

The output for this program is:
(a) 36 5
(b) 0 5
(c) 18 18
(d) 5 5

16. Consider the following statement
s1: A declaration of a variable announces the storage of a variable
s2 : A definition of a variable announces the storage of a variable
Which of the following is true?
(a) s1, s2 is correct
(b) s1 is incorrect s2 is correct
(c) s1 is correct s2 is incorrect
(d) s1, s2 is incorrect

17. Consider the following program divided into three source file main.c , f2.c . f3.c .

main.c

```
void f2() ;
void f3();
static  int a;
static int b ;
main()
{
 f3();
 f2();
 printf("f1=%d f1=%d
", a , b);
}
```

f2.c

```
void f2();
int a ;
int b;
void f2()
{
printf("f2=%d
f2=%d\n" , a , b);
}
```

f3.c

```
void f3();
extern int a;
extern int b;
void f3()
{
 a = 8 ;
 b =9 ;
 printf("f3=%d
f3=%d\n" , a, b);
}
```

The output for this program is:

(a) f3=8 f3= 9
f2=0 f2 =0
f1=0 f1=0

(b) f3=8 f3= 9
f2=8 f2=9
f1=8 f1=9

(c) f3=0 f3= 0
f2=8 f2=9
f1=0 f1=0

(d) None of the above

18. Which of the following is false?

(a) Register declaration can only be applied to automatic variable and to the formal parameters of a function.

(b) Address of a register variable can not be taken

(c) Register declaration can be applied to global variable

(d) None of the above

19. Consider the following program:

```
void f(int );
main( )
{
    f(2);
    f(3);
}

void f( int x)
{
    int  i =x ;
    {
        static i
        i =i ;
        i =i +x ;
        printf("%d\t" , i);
    }
    i = i +x ;
    printf("%d\t" , i) ;
}
```

The output for this program is:
(a) 2 4 5 6
(b) 4 6 7 6
(c) 4 6 6 6
(e) None of teh above

20. Consider the following program:

```
main( )
{
    static a[3] = {1};
    int   b[3] = { 1};

    printf("%d %d" , a[2] , b[2] );
}
```

The output for this program is:
(a) 1 1
(b) 0 undefined
(c) 0 0
(d) undefine undefined

Answer With Detailed Explanations

Test 7

1. (a)

```
10001111 10001111   1u
00000000 10000000   1u << 7
11111111 01111111   ~(1u << 7)
10001111 10001111   i
10001111 00001111   i & = ~( 1u <<7 )
```

2. (b)
if there are fewer initilazier then trailing members are initialized with 0

3. (d)
The first inclusion of std.h defines the name STD ; further inclusion will find the name defined and skip down to the #endif

4. (c)
Program partition the array (partition element is a[0] such that all the number left to 5 is less than 5 and all the number greater than five is right to five

5 (b)

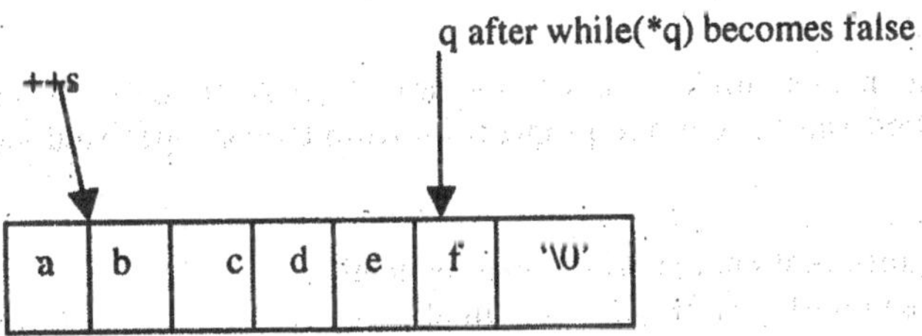

If two pointers to objects of the same type are subtracted, the result is a signed intger value represented the displacement between the pointer to object ;

6. (c)

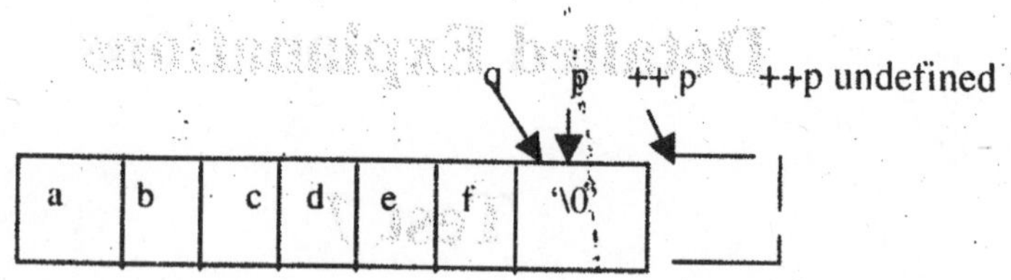

Taking a pointer to the element one beyond the end of an array is certain to work
If p points to the last member of an array then (++p –p) has value 1

7. (b)
local variable x hide scope of global variable int x =x ; assignment of local x that is having undefined value static int y =y ; static variable is initialized with zero always so y is initialized zero

8. (b)
Output of progrm is 11

```
while(i<10) /* while(9<10)*/ {
   ++i; /* becomes  10 */
   for( ;;) {
   if(++i <5) / *  i become 11**/ both for loop and while loop
   terminates now
   continue;
   break;
}
```

9. (b)
First name in an enum has value 0 the next 1 (as A=0 , B=1) .If not all values are Specified , unspecified values continue progression from the last specified values , that is D=6 F=7

10. (d)
Names in different enumeration must be disnict
Example enum e1 { A , B ,C}; enum e2 { A , B ,C} /* in a program is not valid */
Values need not be differen in the same enumeration

```
enum  {  a= 1 ; b =1 , c}  /*  ok   */
```

11. (b)
(3^4(True) && (4^4)(/*4^4 =0 flase*/) || ++a(5)
The operator && and || will not evaluate their second argument unless doing so is required

12. (b)
precedence of operator > , < is higher than <<=
and associativity of operator < > is from left to right
(c>b>)>a) = (1>a)= 0) / * c>b become true hence value is 1)
similarliy a<c<b = ((a<c)<b) evaluate 1
0^1 becomes 1 ; a<< =1 become 4 ;

13. (a)

```
0 0 0 0 0 0 0 0 0 0 0 0 0 0 0 0     i^i
1 1 1 1 1 1 1 1 1 1 1 1 1 1 1 1     ~( i^i)
1 1 1 1 1 1 1 1 1 1 1 1 1 1 0 0     (~( i^i) <<2)
0 0 0 0 0 0 0 0 0 0 0 0 0 0 1 1     (~ (~( i^i) <<2))
0 0 0 0 0 0 0 0 0 0 0 0 1 1 0 0     (~ (~( i^i) <<2))<<2
0 0 0 0 0 0 1 0 0 0 0 0 1 0 0 1     i
0 0 0 0 0 0 1 0 0 0 0 0 1 0 0 1     i^((~ (~( i^i) <<2))<<2)
```

14. (b)

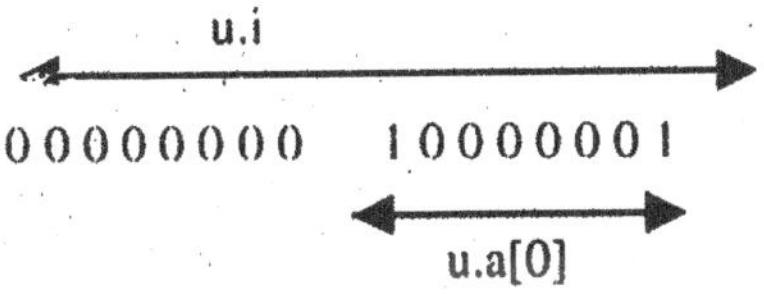

```
  <------------ u.i ------------>
  00000000      10000001
              <--- u.a[0] --->
```

j = u .a[0] & 1 = 00000001 <<7 = 10000000
u .a[0] = u .a[0]>> 1 = 0 1000000 0
u .a[0]= u .a[0] |j = 0 1000000001 10000000=1 1000000
Program rotate u.a[0] one bit right

15. (b)
Only statement belong to case is execute i =3; i*i no effect
Scope of i inside switch is local, storage is static, static variable initialize with 0
case 5 is execute i = i+i = 0+0 ; default executed as there is no break statement i =i+i =0
Inside switch statement printf print 0 for local variable that is having scope with switch block
Outer printf print 5 for varable i that is having scope main block

16. (b)
A declaration of variable announces the type of a variable?

17. (b)
Static declaration of a and b in main.c limit the scope of a and b with main.c file .Same variable name a and b can be used in other file as there would be no conflict with the same names in the other file

18. (c)
Register variable can only be applied to automatic variable and to the formal parameter

19. (a)
Inner loop { i =i is initialized i =0 not i =2(when f(2) is called

Static variable contain their value even though block exit

20. (c)
If there are fewer initializers for an array than the numbers specified, the missing element will be zero for global, static or automatic variable

Test 8

1. Consider the following program:

```
main( )
{
   char arr[][3] = { {'1','2'}, {'4','5'} } ;
   printf("%s", arr+1) ;
}
```

Output for this program is:
(a) 4 5
(b) 2 4 5
(c) 1 2 4 5
(d) None of the above

2. Consider the following program:

```
struct st {
   int a ;
   char b[10] ;
   };
void foo( struct st*);
main( )
{
   struct st ab = { 5 , "ready"} ;
   foo(&ab);
   printf("%d %s", ab.a, ab.b);
}
void foo(struct st *p)
{
   p->a=6 ;
   p->b[4]='e';
}
```

Output for this program is:
(a) 6 ready
(b) 5 reade
(c) 6 reade
(d) 5 ready

3. Consider the following program

```
struct st {
    int a ;
    int b ;
};
void foo( struct st *);
main( )
{
    struct st ab = { 128 , 768} ;
    struct st *pq =&ab;
    foo(pq);
}

void foo(struct st *p)
{
    char *pt;
    p->a =768;
    p->b =128;
    pt= (char*)p ;
    printf("%d" ,*++pt) ;
}
```

Output for this program is:
(a) 1
(b) 2
(c) 3
(d) 4

4. Consider the following program

```
static  int a;
int b;
main( )
{
    int c ;
}
```

Linkage of a, b and c are
(a) internal, external and no linkage respectively
(b) external, external and no linkage respectively
(c) external, internal and no linkage respectively
(d) internal, internal and no linkage respectively

5. Consider the following code segment
```
int a[] = { 1 , 2 3, 4,5 };
```
Correct expression to calculate number of element in array a is
(a) sizeof(a)/ sizeof(*a)
(b) sizeof(a)/ sizeof(a[0])
(c) sizeof(a)/ sizeof(a[1])
(d) all of the above

6. Consider the following program

```
main( )
{
   char *pt , *ptr ;
   pt =(char*) malloc(5);
   strcpy(pt ,"abcd" ) ;
   ptr =( char*)realloc(pt , 10) ;
   ptr = pt ;
   ptr = pt +strlen(pt) ;
   strcpy(ptr   , "ef" ) ;
   printf("%s" ,pt ) ;
}
```

Output for this program is:
(a) abcdef
(b) abcd
(c) efg
(d) None of the above

7. Consider the following declaration

```
typedef int *num ;
const num ptr ;
ptr is
```

(a) Pointer to const integer
(b) ptr is a const pointer to int
(c) ptr is a const pointer to const int
(d) None of the above

8. Consider the following program:

```
main( )
{
   magic(15);
```

```
void magic( int i)
{
    if(i) {
    magic(i/3);
    printf("%c" , "012"[i%3]);
    }
}
```

Output for this program is:
(a) 012
(b) 120
(c) 210
(d) None of the above

9. Consider the following program:

```
main( )
{
    int j ;
    unsigned  int  i= 15 ;
    j =0;
    while(j<16)
        printf("%d"  , (i<<j++ & 0x8000) ? 1 :0  );
}
```

Output for this program is:
(a) 0000000000001111
(b) 1111000000000000
(c) 0000000000000000
(d) 1111111111111111

10. Consider the following program:

```
main( )
{
    int a[][5]={0} ;
    int (*ptr)[5]= a ;
    printf("%d %d" , sizeof(ptr) , sizeof(*ptr) ) ;
}
```

If pointer is 4 byte and int is 4 byte then Output for this program is:
(a) 4 20
(b) 4 4
(c) 20 4
(d) None of the above

11. Consider the following program:

```
main( )
{
   union  {
      struct{
         char c[2] ;
         char ch[2];
      }s;
      struct  {
         int i;
         int j ;
      }st;
   }u = {12, 1};
   printf("%d %d ", u.st.i , u.st.j) ;
}
```

Output for this program is:
(a) 268 0
(b) 12 1
(c) 12 0
(d) 0 268

12. In Q11 if u is initialized as u = {12, 1, 15, 1} then output for the program is:
(a) 15 12
(b) 268 271
(c) 12, 15
(d) None of the above

13. A computer with a 16 bit word size uses 2's complement to represent integers. The range of integers that can be represented by this computer is
(a) -2^{15} to $2^{15}-1$
(b) -2^{16} to 2^{15}
(c) -2^{16} to 2^{16}
(d) None of the above

14. Consider the following program:

```
void foo(int [] ) ;
main( )
{
   static int  i[6];
   foo(i);
   printf("%d %d" ,i[4] ,i[5]);
```

```
}
void foo(int j[] )
{
    j = j +2
    j[3] = 5 ;
}
```

Output for this program is:

(a) 0 5
(b) 0 0
(c) 5 0
(d) None of the above

15. Consider the following program:

```
main( )
{
    char *ptr ="%d%t%s";

    while(*ptr++!='t') ;
    printf(ptr, ptr) ;
 }
```

Output for this program is:

(a) s
(b) %s
(c) %d%t%s
(d) None of the above

16. Consider the following program:

```
main( )
{
    char ar[3] ={'a','b'};
    char arr[] ={'a','b'};
    printf("%s %s" , ar ,arr) ;
}
```

Output for this program is:

(a) ab ab
(b) undefined ab
(c) ab undefined
(d) None of the above

17. Consider the following program:

```
void  foo(int a ,int b ,...);
main( )
{
   foo(1,5);
   foo(2,5,6);
}
void foo( int a,int b, ...)
{
   int j ;
   int *ptr = &b ;
   j=0 ;
   while(j<a) {
   printf("%d " , *ptr);
   ++j ;
   ++ptr ;
   }
}
```

Output for this program is:

(a) 5 5 6
(b) 15 2 5 6
(c) 1 2
(d) None of the above

18. Consider the following program:

```
void  foo( int i ,char* b ,...);
main( )
{
   foo(2,"bb","aa");
}
void foo( int a, char* b, ...)
{
   int j ;
   char *ptr = b ;
   j=0 ;
   while(j<a) {
      printf("%s " , ptr);
      ++j ;
      ++ptr ;
   }
```

Output for this program is:

(a) bb b

(b) bb aa

(c) bb

(d) bb aa

19. Consider the following program:

```
#if i^i
#error "in praise of error"
#endif
main( )
{
   printf("in praise of printf") ;
}
```

Output for this program is:

(a) in praise of printf

(b) in praise of error

(c) erro in praise of error

(d) not compile

20. Consider the following program:

```
#if ~(i^i)
#error "in praise of error"
#endif
main( )
{
   printf("in praise of printf") ;
}
```

Output for this program is:

(a) in praise of printf

(b) in praise of error

(c) both (a) and (b)

(d) not compile(#error in praise of error)

Answer With Detailed Explanations

Test 8

1. (a)

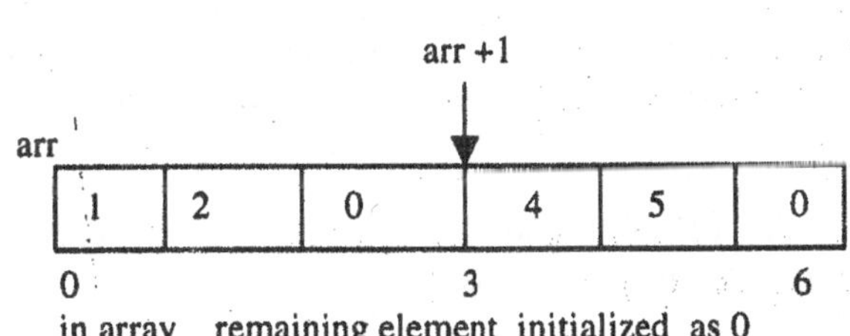

2. (c)
Address of structure is passed and change in function foo reflects change in a and b

3. (c)

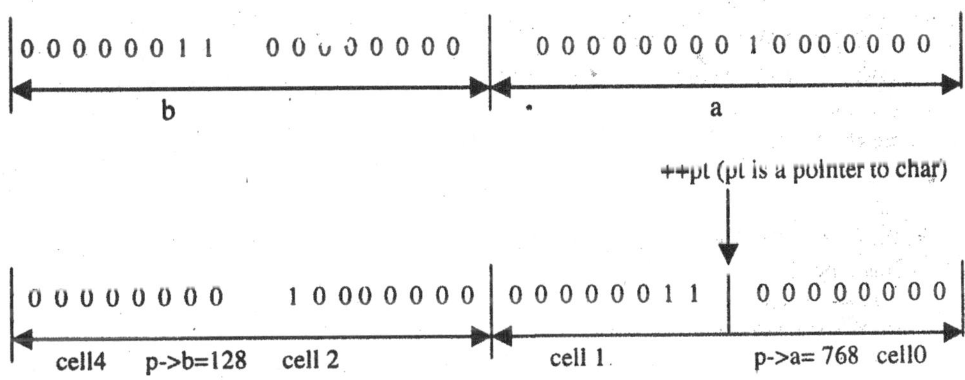

4. (a)
If the external declaration for a variable include the static specifier, the variable has internal linkage so a has internal linkage other wise it has external linkage as b has external linkage. if a declaration for a variable within a block does not include the extern specifier , then the variable has no linkage so c has no linkage
Linkage :Within a source file (translation unit) all declaration of the same variable with internal linkage refer to the same variable and variable is unique to that source file

For external linkage all declaration for the same variable refer to the same thing, and variable is shared by the entire program

5. (d)
Number of element in a array is sizeof array divide by sizeof one element

6. (a)
Reallocates main memory
Syntax:
```
void *realloc(void *block, size_t size);
```
Attempts to shrink or expand the previously allocated block to size bytes. Returns the address of the reallocated block, which can be different than the original address. If the block cannot be reallocated or size ==0, realloc returns NULL.

7. (b)
const modify the type of ptr and ptr is a pointer so pt is a const pointer to int example (as const int p) declare p is a const int

8. (b)
Convert int to ternary $(15)_{10} = (120)_3$
first divide the number by 3 test it for none zero if number is not zero call magic again other wise printf("%c" , "012"[i%3]) will show a ternary digit
i % 3 evaluates to an integer between 0 to 3 . The program uses this value as a subscript for a character string that ternary point to

```
 "012"[15%3]  =  "012"[0]  = 0
next  "012"[5%3]  =  "012"[2]  = 2  /*  "012" is a  array of
character
next " 012"[1%3]  = 1 / * terminates */
```

9. (a)
Program print binary equivalent of i
Idea here is
1000000000000000 (this is selected for masking)
0000000000001111 (15)
for each (15)iteration 15 is shifted to right and & with 0x8000 if it is one the one is printed else 0

10. (a)
int (*ptr)[5]= a ;
ptr yield size of pointer that is 4
*ptr pointer to array of five int ptr is size of array

11. (a)

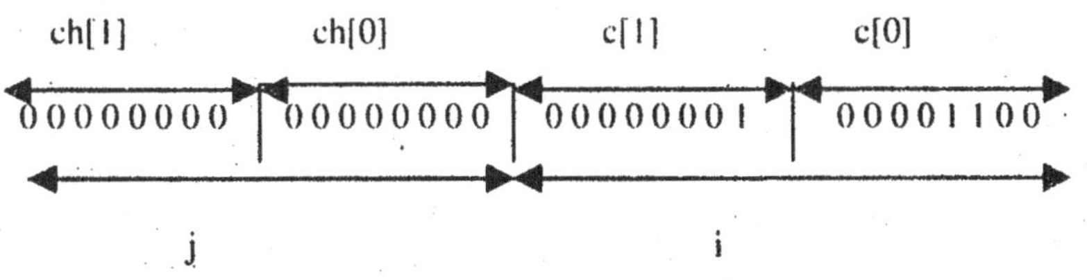

u.st.i = 00000001 00001100 = $(268)_{10}$
u.st.j = 00000000 00000000 = 0

12. (b)

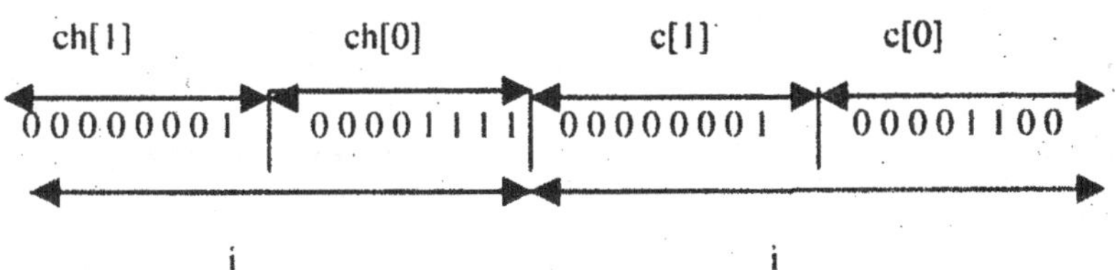

u.st.i = 00000001 00001100 = $(268)_{10}$
u.st.j = 00000001 00001111 = $(271)_{10}$

13. (a)
the range of integers that can be represented in 2's complement in a 16 –bit word is
-2^{15} to $2^{15}-1$ /* range is $-2^{n-1} <= n <= 2^{n-1} - 1$ */

14. (a)
When array is used as a function argument it decay into pointer
foo(int j[]) becomes foo(int *j)
Passing array name to function means address of its first element is passed &i[0]
static array initialized to 0

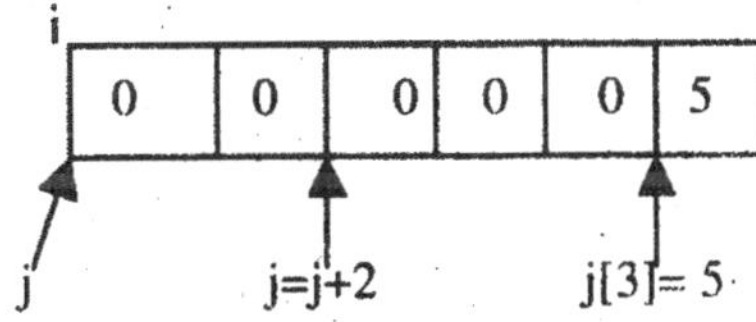

Change reflect in i[5] because address is passed to function

15. (b)

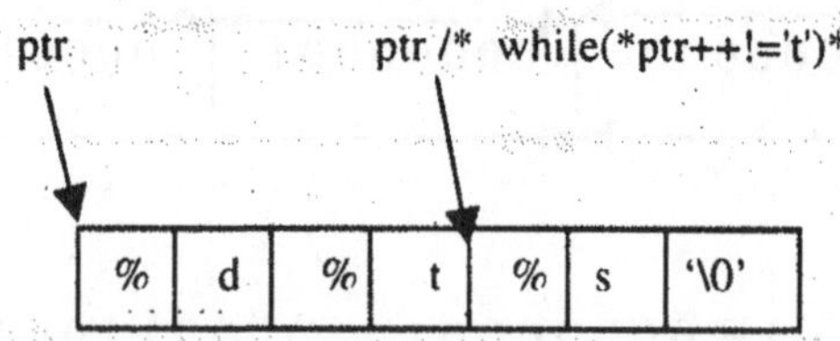

printf("%s" ,"%s") ; print /* %s */

16. (c)
in ar[3] remaining element initialize 0 (a[2]=0) terminated by null)
arr has two elements (not terminated by null)

17. (a)
ptr contain addres of b that is 1004 and ++ptr point next address too 1006 an so on

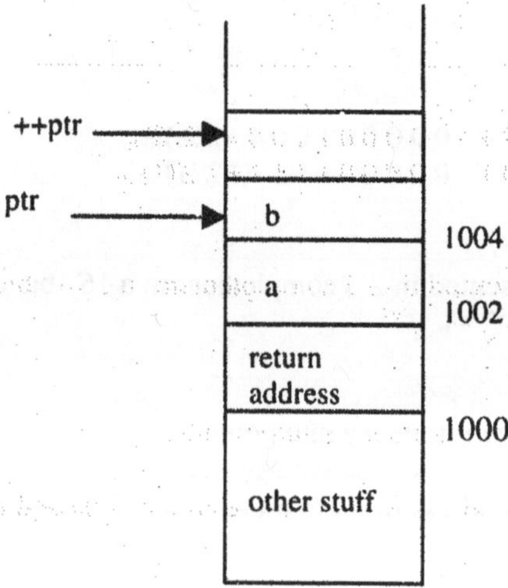

18. (a)
in this case ptr is pointing to char

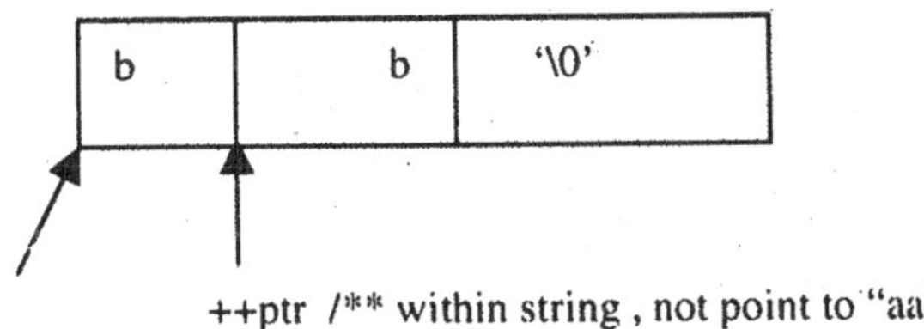

printf("s" , ptr) /*** print bb

Next iteration prinntf("%s , ptr·) /* print b and loop terminate ***

19 (a)
#if i^i becomes 0 and #error directive not executed

20 (d)
#error cause the preprocessor to write error message

Test 9

State true or false for the following question

1. #define MACRO(test) # test

```
main( )
{
    printf(MACRO(magic));
}
```

This program prints magic

2. Data area is divided into two parts initialized data uninitialized data
3. Initialized data area is sometimes called BSS(block started by symbol)
4. System fills the bss area with zero
5. Stack is a place for compiler to store automatic variable
6. System can't determine size of the stack before program runs
7. C program usually don't access the text area unless you use pointer to function
8. Using the name of a function without parenthesis makes the compiler interpret it as a pointer
9. Location of constant string in memory (text area or data area) may be compiler dependent
10. If automatic variable are not initialize their values are zero
11. C limit the destination of a goto to within the same function
12. By using setjmp and longjmp you can transfer program control to a different function
13. Address of register variable can be determined
14. A string has type array of int
15. Expression ptr->point is same as (*ptr).point
16. An array type of unknown size is known as incomplete type
17. void v ; object type void can not be declared

18. Address of a bit field member of a structure or union can be taken

19. sizeof bit field can't be determined

20. While(1) { } is not equivalent to for {; ;}

Answer With Detailed Explanations

Test 9

1. (True)
   # Operators makes quotation MACRO (magic) yields "magic"

2. (True)

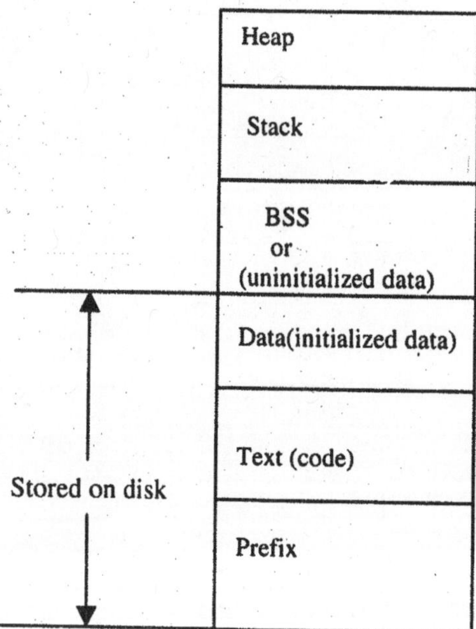

Typical subdivision of run time memory into code and data

3. (False)
   see explanation 2

4. (True)
   see explanation 2

5. (True)

6. (True)
System can't determine size of the stack before program runs

7. (True)

8. (True)
```
int f();
int (*P) () = f;
```

9. (True)
String may be placed in data area or text area depend upon implementation

10. (False)
If automatic variable are not initialize theirs values are not known

11. (True)

12. (True)
See explanation 1 of test 1

13. (False)
Address of register variable can not be determined

14. (False)
A string has type array of int and storage static

15. (True)

16. (True)
An array type of unknown size is known as incomplete type

17. (True)
Object of type void can't be declared

18. (False)
Address of bit field can't be taken

19. (True)
sizeof bit field can't be determined

20. (False)
While(1) { } is equivalent to for {;;;}
For (expr1 ; expr2; expr3) if expr1 or expr3 is omitted , it is simply dropped from the expansion if the test expr2 is not present , it is taken as permanently true so for (;;) { } is an infinite loop also while(1) { } is infinite loop

Test 10

State true or false for the following question

1. An array can be expressed as a pointer and offset.

2. f(char p[]) and f(char *p) is always equivalent.

3. ++*p are eqivalent to (*p)++ and *p++

4. A static variable is initialized only the first time the block is enter

5. consider following macro #define

```
div(z) = (z/z)
```

if z>0 then what ever be the formal parameter it always gives one

6. Array size must be specified with the definition int a[10] and with the an external declaration extern a[10];

7. Default return of function type is int ;

8. while ((c = getchar()) != 'a') is equivalent to (c =getchar() != 'a')

9. In C all variable must be declared before they are used

10. If an arithmetic operator has one floating operand and one integer operand then the integer will be converted to floating point before the operation is done.

11. In all cases printf(ptr) and printf("%s" , ptr); print the same string(where ptr point address of string)

12. Static declaration(static int f( );)can not be used for function

13. Static declaration can not be applied to local variable

14. if (!p) is equivalent to p ?0:1

15. if(!p) is equivalent to if(p!=0)

16. sizeof(3.4) is equivalent to sizeof(float)

17. cases and default clause can occur in any order

18. External and static variable are initialized to zero by default

19. String constants "real ," "time" is equivalent to "real, time"

20. 'y' is same as "y"

Answer With Detailed Explanations

Test 10

1. (True)
`a[i] = *(a+i)`

2 True
in function char p[] decay into pointer so char p [] is equivalen char*p

3. False
++*p ,(*p)++ both increments what it points
*p++ increments p instead of what it points

4. True

5. False
`div( (3 +3) = 3 +3/3+3 = 7`
Remember substitution of macro are made only for tokens and not take place within quoted string

6. False
Array size is optional with an external declaration

7. True
If no prototype is specified for function then default return is int

8. False
The precedence of ! = is higher than that of = which means that in the absence of the parentheses the relational test != would be done before the assignment c = getchar != 'a' is eqivalent to c= (getchar()!= 'a') which is differ from (c = =getchar()) !='a')

9 True
Before use variable must be declared in C

10. True
According to arithmetic conversion rule
if one operand is float and other is int the other is converted to float

11. False
printf (ptr) fails if ptr contains %
example printf("a%cb") , printf("%s" , "a%cb") print different string

12. False
If a function is declared static its name is invisible outside of the file in which it is declared.

13. False
static variable that are local remain exist rather than coming and going each time the function is activated

14. (True)

15. (False)
if(!p) is equivalent to if(p==0)

16. (False)
sizeof(3.4) is equivalent to sizeof(double) by default floating–point constants is double unless suffixed. . The suffixes f or F indicates a float constant.

17. (True)

```
switch(i)

{
   default  :  statement;    //ok
   case     : statement  ;
}
```

```
switch(I)
    {
    case : statement   ;
    default : statement ;    //ok
    }
```

18. (True)
External and static variable are initialized to zero by default

19. (True)
Adjacent string literals are concatenated into a single string

20. (False)
'y' is an integer . "y" is an array of character

Test 11

For all the problem consider the following node type

```
typedef   Struct   link{
   char a[6] ;
   struct link *next;
   }node ;
```

1. Let ptr is a pointer variable that points to the next free node in a singly linked list of free (available) nodes. If p points to a node currently being accessed in a program, then the program fragment

```
if (p == null)    printf("error");
else
{
   p->next = ptr;
ptr = p;
}
```

(a) Creates a new node by removing a node from the free node list
(b) Remove p by insertion it into the front of the available node list
(c) Exchange the node to which p and ptr are pointing
(d) None of the above

2. Let ptr be a pointer to some node in a linked list L as given in fig 1 .Let pptr be the node preceding ptr.

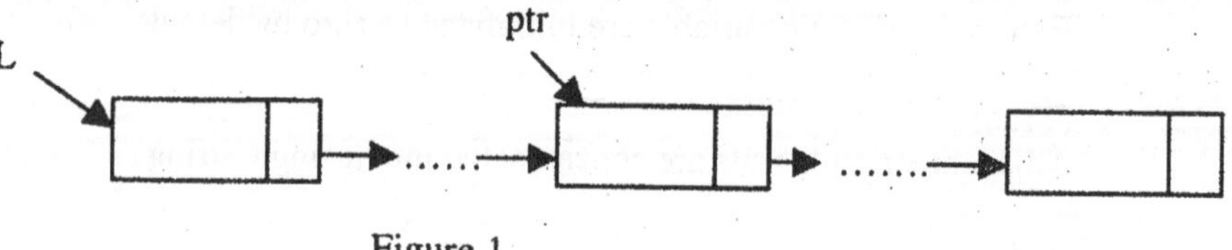

Figure 1

Which of the following code deletes node ptr from L

(a) if(!pptr) L =L->next ;
else pptr->next=ptr->next;

(b) if(pptr) L =L->next ;
else ptr->next=pptr->next;

(c) if(pptr) L =L->next ;
else pptr->next=ptr->next;

(d) if(!pptr) L =L->next ;
else pppt=ptr->next;

3. Let ptr be a pointer to a single linked list as in fig. 2 .Let nptr be a pointer to some arbitrary node in the list.

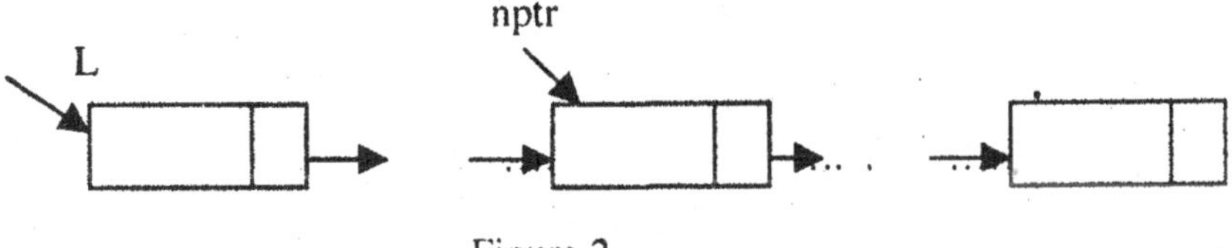

Figure 2

Which of the following code insert a node q following the node at nptr.
Node Structure is given as

```
node * q = (node*)malloc(sizeof(node)) *****?
```

(a) if (L) { L =q ; q->next= 0}
else {q->next = nptr ; nptr->next = q}

(b) (a) if (!L) { L =q ; q->next= 0}
else {q = nptr->next ; nptr->next = q}

(c) (a) if (!L) { L =q ; q->next= 0}
else {q->next = nptr->next ; nptr->next = q}

(c) None of the above

Consider the two-linked list as given in figure 3

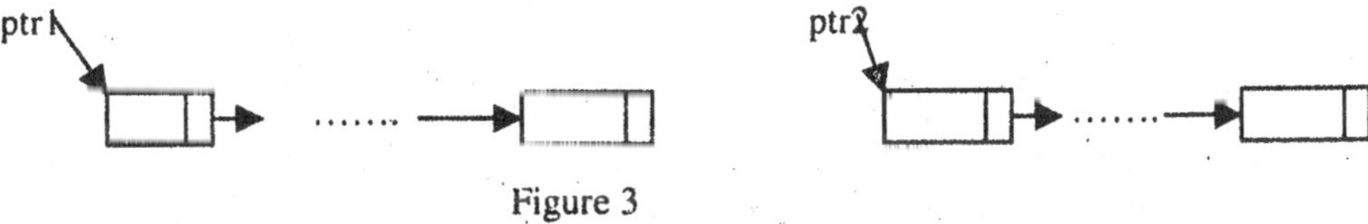

Figure 3

correct code to concatenate L1 and L2 such as is

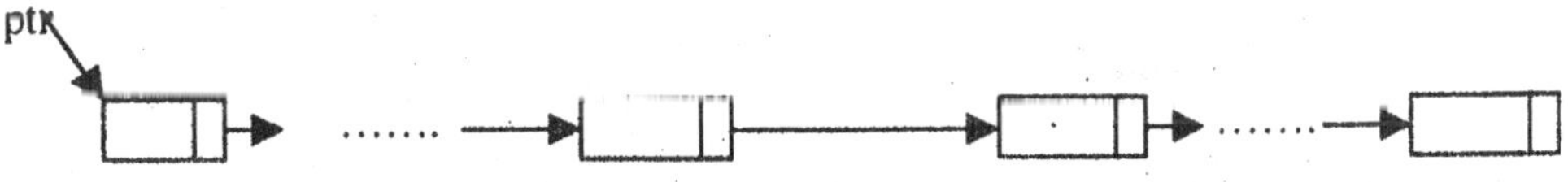

All node ptr1, ptr2 and ptr , pt are type node

(a)
```
ptr=ptr1 ;
If(ptr1) ptr=ptr2 ; return ;
If (ptr2) return ;
pt =ptr1 ;
While (pt->next) pt =pt->next;
```

```
pt->next = ptr2 ;
```

(b)
```
ptr=ptr1 ;
If(!ptr1) ptr=ptr2 ; return ;
If (!ptr2) return ;
pt =ptr1 ;
While (pt) pt =pt->next;
pt->next = ptr2 ;
```

(c)
```
ptr=ptr1 ;
If(!ptr1) ptr=ptr2 ; return ;
If (!ptr2) return ;
pt =ptr1 ;
While (pt->next) pt =pt->next;
pt->next = ptr2 ;
```

(d)
```
ptr=ptr1 ;
If(!ptr1) ptr=ptr2 ; return ;
If (!ptr2) return ;
pt =ptr1 ;
While (pt->next) pt =pt->next;
pt->next = ptr1 ,
```

5. Consider the following circular list as shown in figure 4

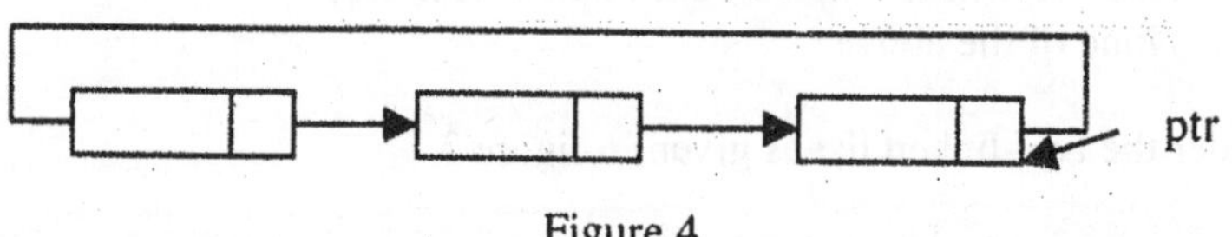

Figure 4

correct code to insert node pt(node *pt) in front of the circular list ptr. ptr points to the last node

(a) `if(ptr) { pt = ptr ; ptr->next = pt };`
`else { ptr->next = pt->next ; pt->next = ptr };`

(b) `if(!ptr) { ptr = pt ; pt->next = ptr };`
`else { ptr->next = pt->next ; pt->next = ptr };`

(c) `if(!ptr) { ptr = pt ; pt->next = ptr };`
`else { pt->next = ptr->next ; ptr->next = pt };`

(d) None of the above

6. A doubly linked list structure is defined as .

```
    struct link{
        int   item;
        struct link *prev ;
        struct link *next;
} node ;
```

node *p ; /* assume p is allocated memory */
let pointer pt points to an element in the list as shown in figure 5 .

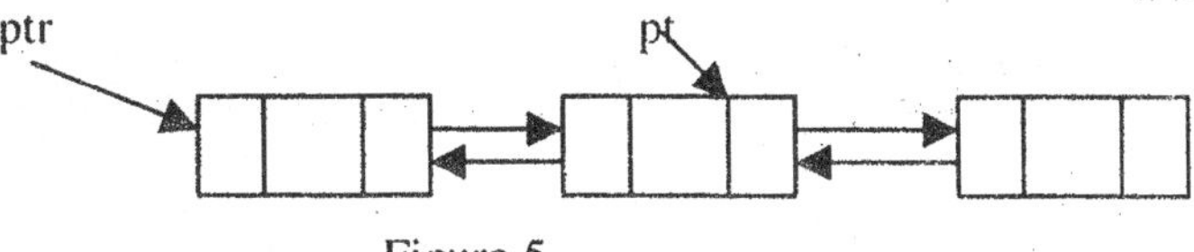

Figure 5

Which of the following code fragment would correctly insert a new node, pointed to by pointer p to the right of pt

(a)
```
p->next = pt->next
p->prev =pt;
pt->next =p;
p->next->prev = p ;
```
(b)
```
p->prev = pt
p->next =pt->next;
pt->next=p ;
p->next->prev = pt ;
```
(c)
```
p->next = pt->next
p->prev =pt->next;
p->next->prev = pt;
pt->next = p ;
```
(d) None of the above

7. A doubly linked list structure is defined as above. A pointer pt points to an element in the list as shown in figure 6 .

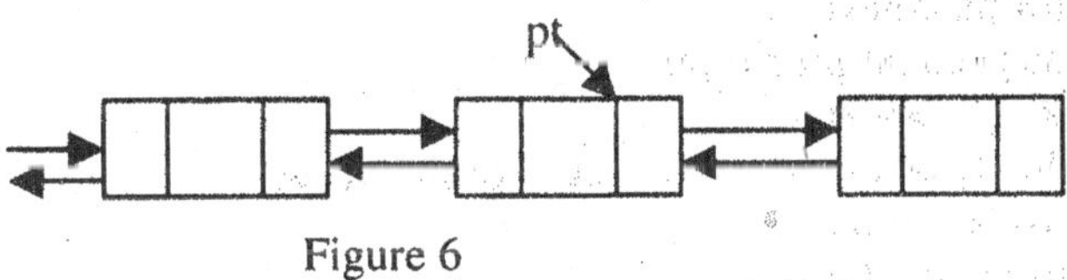

Figure 6

Which of the following code fragment would correctly delete node pt

(a)
```
node * ptr =pt;
ptr->next->prev= ptr->prev;
free(ptr) ;
ptr->prev->next=ptr->next
free(ptr) ;
```
(b)
```
node * ptr =pt;
ptr->next->prev= ptr->prev;
ptr->prev->next=ptr->prev
free(ptr) ;
```

(c) node * ptr =pt; .
ptr->next->prev= ptr->prev;
ptr->prev->next=ptr->next
free(ptr) ;

(d) none of the above

8. Consider following linked list. Let ptr points to linked list as shown in figure 7

```
typedef  struct  link{
   unsigned int  i ;
   struct link *next
}node ;
```

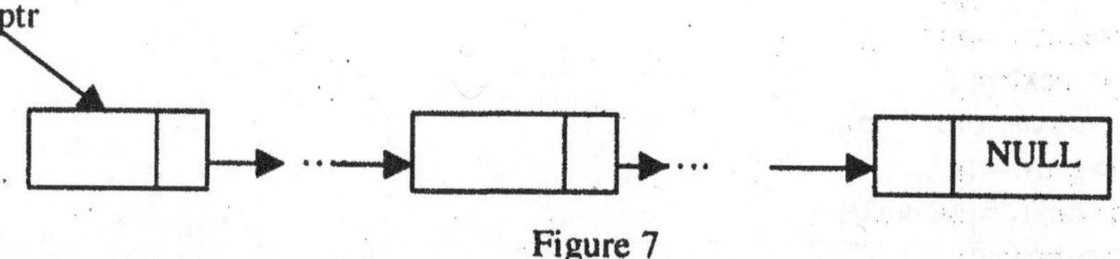

Figure 7

Which of the following code fragment will product all the integers in the linked list (assume that all integers are greater than zero)

(a) unsigned int prod = ptr->i;
ptr= ptr->next ;
while(p) { prod = prod*(ptr->i) ;
ptr= ptr->next ; }

(b) unsigned int prod =0
ptr= ptr->next ;
while(p) { prod = prod*(ptr->i) ;
ptr= ptr->next ; }

(c) unsigned int prod = ptr->i;
ptr= ptr->next ;
while(p->next->next) { prod = prod*(ptr->i) ;
ptr= ptr->next ; }

(d) unsigned int prod = ptr->i;
ptr= ptr->next ;
while(p) { prod = prod*(ptr->i) ;
ptr= ptr->next->next ; }

9. Consider the following code segment used to sum the coefficient of any two non empty polynomials where the term of the polynomial are kept in a linked list

```
struct poly {
   int  exp;
   double  coeff ;
```

```
   struct poly *next;
} ;
struct poly  sum 1, sum2,   * current; result ;
sum(struct poly * sum 1 , struct poly * sum2 )
{
   struct poly * tempm , *t;
   struct poly  *p = sum1;
   struct poly  *q= sum2 ;
   temp = malloc( sizeof ( struct poly));
   current =  temp;
   while( p  && q) {
   current->coeff = p->coeff + q->.coeff
   t =current;
   p = p->next;
   q = q->next;
   current = malloc( sizeof poly))
   t->next = current;
   }
   t->next = null;
   free (current);
}
```

Which of the following is false.

(a) The code gives desired result if the two polynomials are of the same length

(b) The code gives the desired result if terms with matching exponents are located in the same relative nodes of the two linked lists

(c) Code segment produces desired result even if two polynomials are not of the same length

(d) None of the above

10. Consider following circular linked list .Let ptr points to linked list as shown in figure 8

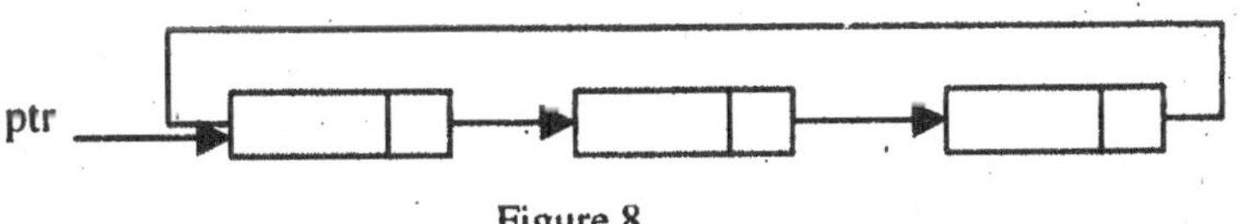

Figure 8

Correct code to find the length of the circular list is(ptr is of type node)
/* count is used to contain the number of length ***/

(a) unsigned int count =0 ;
if(ptr) {
node *pt = ptr ;
do {

```
++count ;
pt ==pt->next ;
} while(pt ==ptr) ;
```

(b)
```
unsigned int count =0 ;
if(ptr) {
node *pt = ptr ;
while(pt==ptr){
++count ;
pt ==pt->next ;
} ;
```

(c)
```
unsigned int count =0 ;
if(ptr) {
node *pt = ptr ;
do {
++count ;
pt ==pt->next ;
} while(pt->next ==ptr) ;
```

(d) None of the above

11. Consider the following code segment in C to traverse a binary tree using the postorder

```
typedef struct tree {
    int   info ;
    struct *left ;
    struct *right ;
}node ;

void postorder(node *tree)
{
    if(t)
    {
        s1;
        s2
        s3
    }
}
```

Statement s1, s2, and s3 should be

(a)
```
postorder(tree->right);
postorder(tree->left);
printf("%d" , tree->info) ;
```

(b)
```
postorder(tree->left);
postorder(tree->right);
printf("%d" , tree->info) ;
```

(c)
```
postorder(tree->left);
```

```
printf("%d" , tree->info) ;
postorder(tree->left);
```

(d)
```
printf("%d" , tree->info)
postorder(tree->left);
postorder(tree->right);
```

12. Consider the following linked list. Let ptr be point to linked list as shown in figure 9

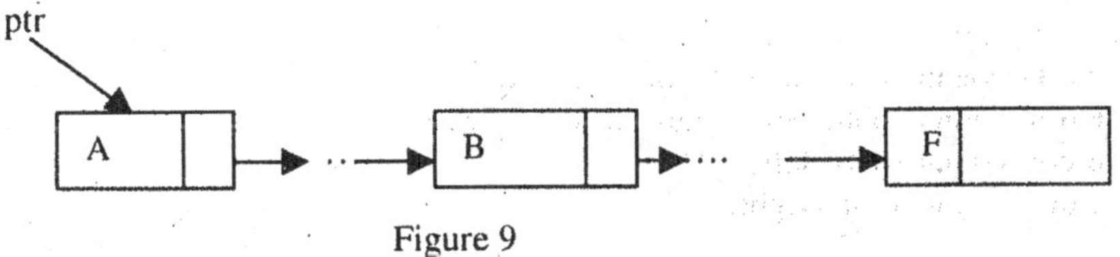

Figure 9

Correct code to traverse linked list in reverse order is (i.e. F, B ......A)
Node type is defined as

```
typedef  Struct  link{
   char i ;
   struct link *next;
}node ;
```

(a)
```
void traverse(node*ptr){
if(ptr) traverse(ptr->next->next);
printf("%c" ,ptr->i) ;
```

(b)
```
void traverse(node*ptr){
if(!ptr) traverse(ptr->next);
printf("%c" ,ptr->i) ;
```

(c)
```
void traverse(node*ptr){
if(ptr) { traverse(ptr->next);
printf("%c" ,ptr->i)} ;
```

(d)
```
void traverse(node*ptr){
if(ptr) traverse(ptr->next);
printf("%c" ,ptr->i) ;
```

13. consider the following code to count the number of node in the binary tree

```
struct tree {
   char a;
   struct btree *left ;
   struct btree *left ;
 } root;
 int count( node *root)
{
```

```
    if(!root) return 0;

        s1

    else
}
```

Statement s1 should be as

(a) return(count(root->left) +count(root->right) +1);
(b) return(count(root->left) +count(root->right));
(c) return(count(root->left) +1);
(d) return(count-(root->right) +1);

14. Consider the following linked list. Let ptr point to linked list as shown in figure 10

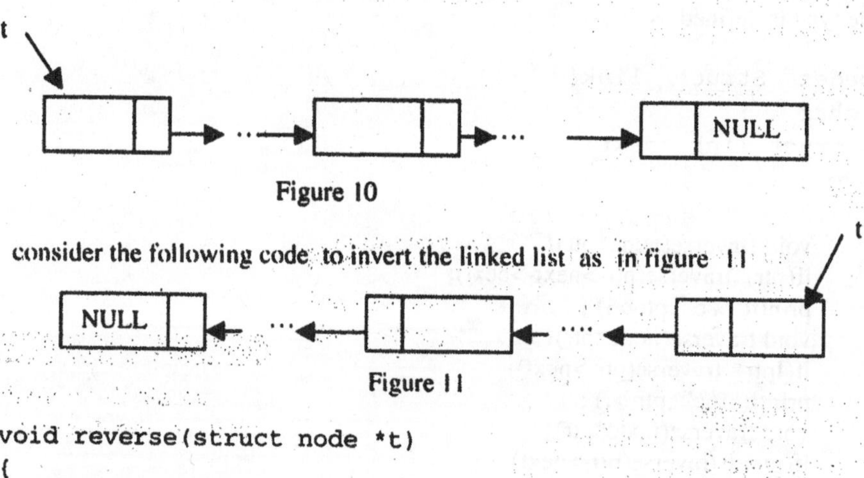

Figure 11

```
void reverse(struct node *t)
{
   struct node *p;
   struct node *r =t ;
   struct node *q = NULL ;
   while( r) {
      p =q ;
      q =r ;
      r = r->next ;
        s1
   }
      t =q ;
}
```

statement s1 should be as

(a) q->next = p;
(b) q->next = r;
(c) p->next = q;
(d) q->next =p->next

15. Consider the following linked list. Let ptr be a pointer point to linked list as shown in figure 12

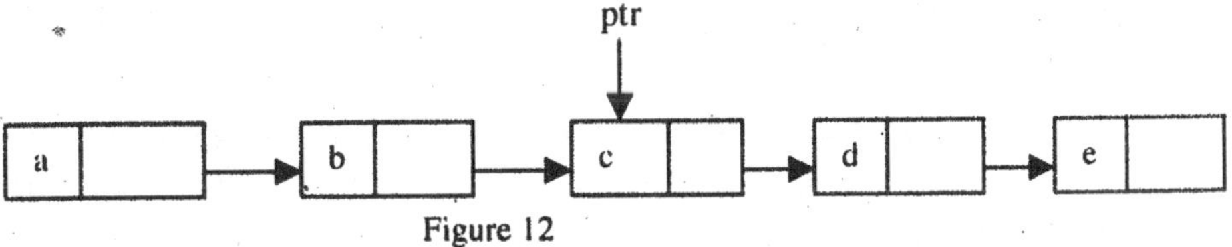

Figure 12

(i) Write a function to insert a node(q) before the node ptr of a linked list when only pointer ptr is given.

(ii) Write a function to delete the node ptr from a linked list when only pointer ptr is given

```
node type is defined as
typedef struct link {
   char ch;
   struct *next ;
} node ;
```

Answer With Detailed Explanations

Test 11

1. (b)
Code adds the node pointed to by p to the free list of nodes pointed to by ptr provided that p is not NULL.

2. (a)
```
if(!pptr) L =L->next  ;  /* remove the first node */
else  pptr->next=ptr->next; /* remove the interior node */
```

3. (c)

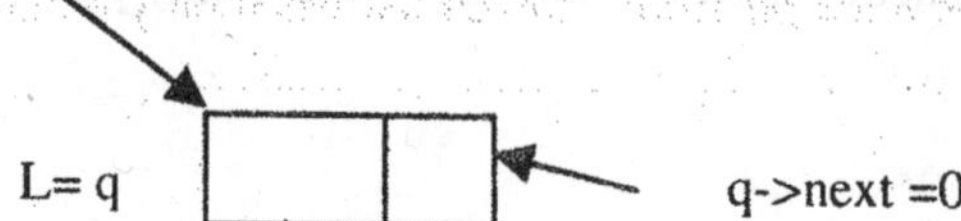

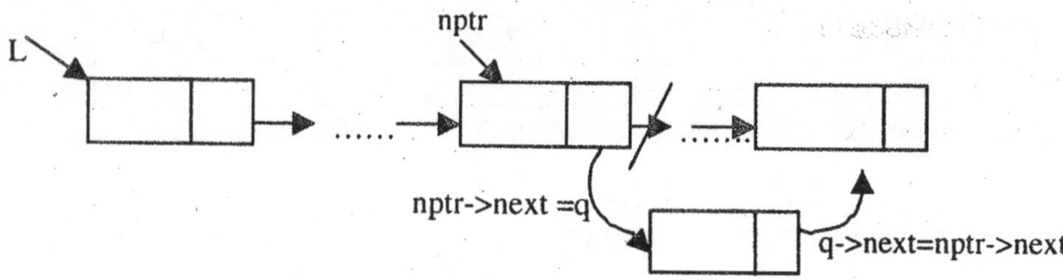

4. (c)
```
ptr = ptr1;
if (ptr1== 0) /**or if(!ptr1)  *
```

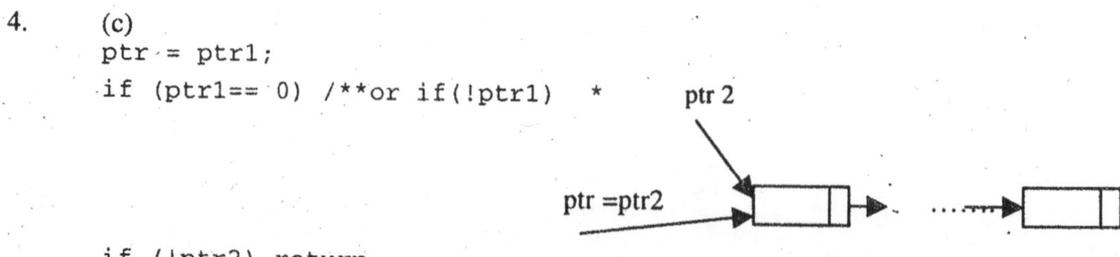


```
if (!ptr2) return
```

```
pt =ptr1;
traverse ptr1 untill   pt->next is null
then  assign pt->next = ptr2
```

5 (c)

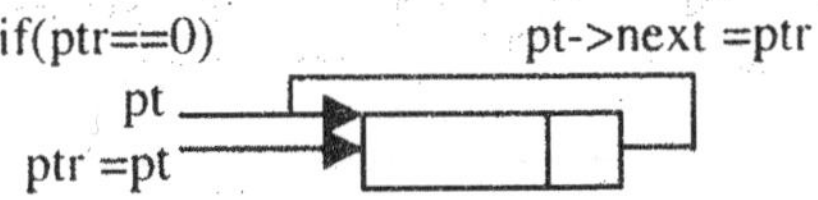

else

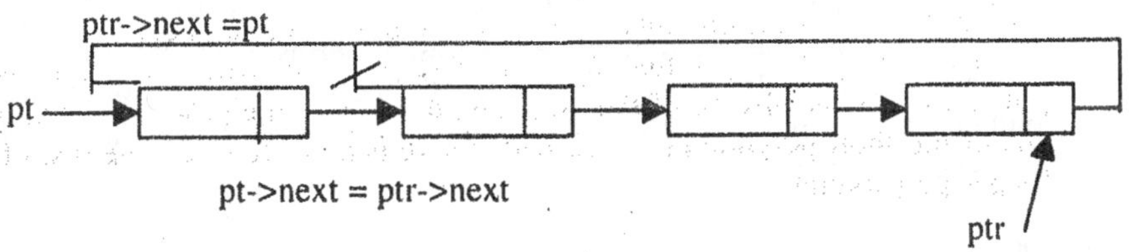

6. (a)

```
c1 :p->next = pt->next
c2 :p->prev  =pt;
c3 :t->next =p;
c4 :p->next->prev = p ;
```

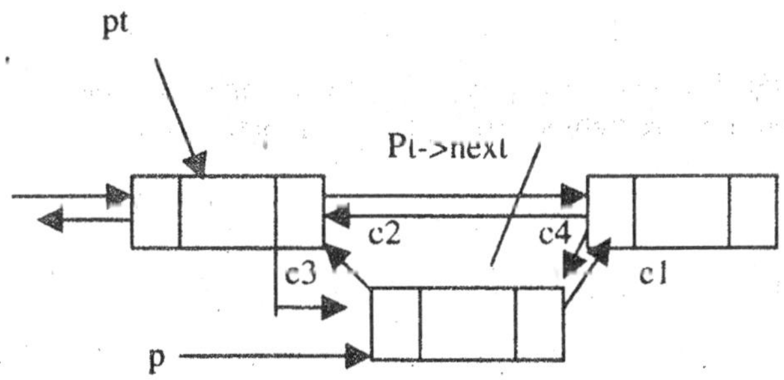

7. (c)

```
* ptr =pt;
c1 :ptr->next->prev= ptr->prev;
c2 :ptr->prev->next=ptr->next
c3 :free(ptr) ;
```

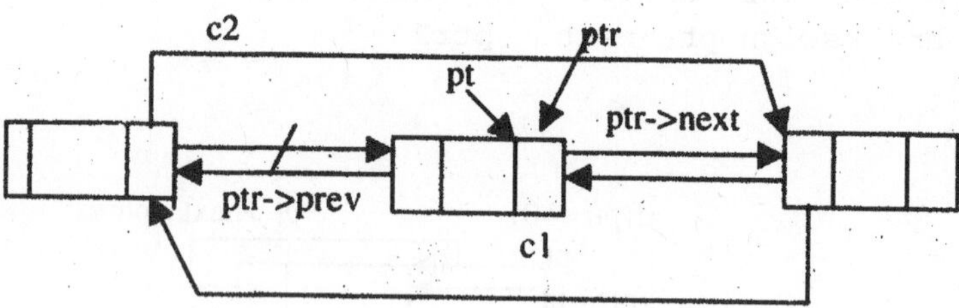

8. (a)

9. (c)
The function sum assume that the terms of the two polynomials are inserted into the link list in such a way that parallel nodes represent terms with the same exponents. The two polynomials must also be of the same length because the procedure terminates as soon as the end of the short polynomial is reached. There is no code to get the rest of the terms from the longer polynomial

10 (a)

11. (b)
pstorder visit is
- -left branch
- -right branch
- -node

12. (d)

13. (a)
number of node in a binary tree is equal to the number of nodes in the left subtree plus number of nodes in the right subtree plus 1(/*root*/)

14 (a)

```
/ *first iteration */
q =NULL ;
{
p =NULL ;
q =r ;
r = r->next ;
q->next = p;

}
```

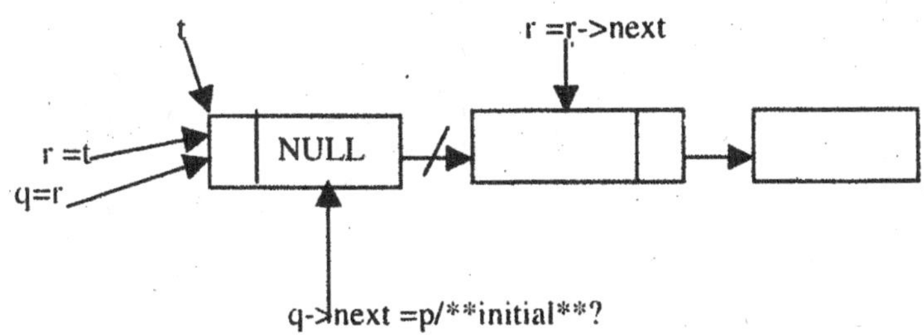


```
/* second iteration/
p =q ;
=r ;
= r->next ;
->next = p;}
```

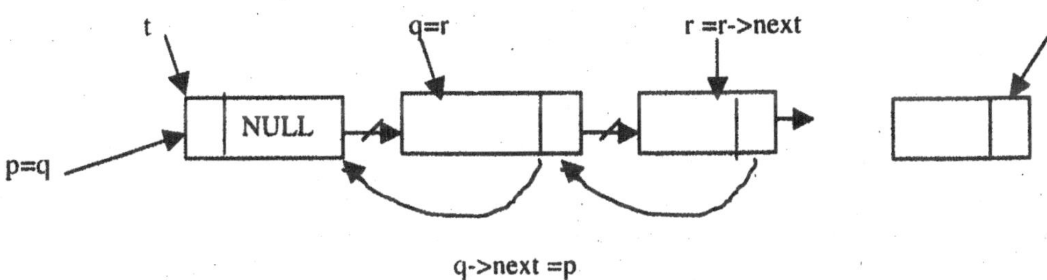

similarly for other iteration finally assign t =q ;

15. (i)

```
void insert( struct node * ptr , char  data)
{
node*q ; / q = (node*) malloc(sizeof(node))
```

/* first insert the new node after ptr , then copy the data field that ptr point to the new node and then put the new data fields into ptr points to */

```
q->next =ptr->next ;   / * insert new node after ptr */
ptr->next= q ;
q->ch = ptr->ch ; /* copy data field of ptr  to new node data
field */
ptr->ch =  data ;    / * copy  new data  to pt->ch       */
}
```

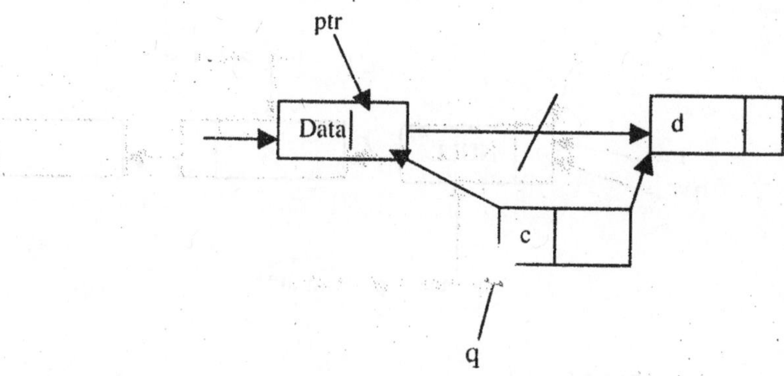

(ii) void delete (struct node*ptr)

```
{
    /*.    copy the  data of node after( ptr->next) to ptr then
    delete  node  after ptr    */
    ptr->ch = ptr->next->ch;
    ptr = ptr->next;
    free(ptr);
}
```

Test 12

1. A solution to the critical section code must satisfy following requirements.
   (a) Mutual exclusion
   (b) Progress
   (c) Bound waiting
   (d) All of the above

2. Let m[0].......m[3] be mutex (binary semaphore) and p[0] ....p[3] be process . Suppose each process execute the following

```
lock(m[i]          ;
lock(m[(i+1)  mod 3] ;

unlock(m[i]);
unlock (m[(i+1)  mod 3]);
```

   This could cause
   (a) Thrashing
   (b) Starvation, but not deadlock
   (c) Deadlock
   (d) None of the above

3. For priority inversion to occur, the system has at least
   (a) Three tasks
   (b) Two tasks
   (c) Four tasks
   (d) Five tasks

4. A situation where a low-priority tasks acts as though it has a higher priority than a high-priority task is called
   (a) Aging
   (b) Priority inversion
   (c) Starvation
   (d) Deadlock

5. Priority Inheritance is a technique to solve
   (a) Deadlock
   (b) Priority inversion
   (c) Starvation
   (d) Shared resource

6. Which of the following is false?
   (a) Semaphore is not owned by a specific task

(b) Priority inheritance can not be implemented for semaphore
(c) Any task can increment a semaphore count by releasing it
(d) A mutex is not owned by a specific task

7. A deadlock situation occur if and only if the following conditions hold
(a) Mutual exclusion and nonpreemption
(b) Circular wait
(c) Hold and wait
(d) All of the above

8. Which of the following is false?
(a) Critical section are not source of priority inversion
(b) Critical sections are source of priority inversion
(c) Critical section are needed to ensure data integrity in program using shared memory
(d) None of the above

9. Which of the following is false
(a) Priority inheritance can lead to deadlock
(b) Priority inheritance prevents deadlock
(c) Priority ceiling protocol prevents deadlock
(d) Priority ceiling allows avoiding the problem of priority inversion

10. A real time system has interrupts A, B, C and D with A being highest –priority device and D being lowest, worst case interrupt latency for device A is
(a) First A interrupts, then B, then C, then D
(b) First D interrupts, then A, then B, then C
(c) First D interrupts, then C, then B, then A
(d) All four devices interrupt simultaneously

11. For a given set of n periodic tasks, the deadline driven scheduling algorithm is feasible if and only if

(a) $\sum_{i=1}^{n} c_i / t_i = 1$

(b) $\sum_{i=1}^{n} c_i / t_i >= 1$

(c) $\sum_{i=1}^{n} c_i / t_i <= 1$

(d) None of the above

Where c_i is the computation time of task i and t_i is its period.

12. Banker's algorithm can be used in
    (a) Deadlock avoidance
    (b) Deadlock prevention
    (c) Deadlock detection and recovery from deadlock
    (d) Prevention and recovery from deadlock

13. Technique best suited for embedded real time system when the number of real –time tasks is unknown is
    (a) MFT (multiprogramming with fixed number of task)
    (b) Swapping
    (c) Overlay's
    (d) MVT (multiprogramming with variable number of task)

14. Source of interrupt latency is
    (a) Propagation delay
    (b) Macroinstruction execution times
    (c) Interrupt disabled
    (d) All of the above

15. Which of the following is false
    (a) A reentrant function may not use variable in a non atomic way unless they are stored on the stack of the task that called the function or are other wise the private variable of that task
    (b) A reentrant function may not call any other function that are not themselves reentrant
    (c) A reentrant function may not use the hardware in a non-atomic way
    (d) A reentrant function may call any other function that are not themselves reentrant

16. Is given function is reentrant?

```
int  j;
void f(void )
{
   if (j>10)
   {
      j=j+1 ;
      printf("%d" , j);
   }
   else
   {
      j=j-1 ;
      printf("%d" , j);
   }
}
```

17. A computer system has 50 megabytes of program memory that is loaded at 70 %, 30 megabytes of RAM area that is loaded at 30%, and 10 megabytes of stack area that is loaded at 60 %. The total memory loading is
(a) 45%
(b) 50%
(c) 49.5 %
(d) 57%

18. A real tine system has interrupts A, B, C and D, with A being highest –priority device and D being lowest, worst case interrupt latency for device D is
(a) First A interrupts, then B, then C, then D
(b) First D interrupts, then A, then B, then C
(c) First D interrupts, then C, then B, then A
(d) All four devices interrupt simultaneously

19. Suppose P_T is the interrupt latency due to propagation delay of the interrupt signal IC_T is the longest completion time for current instruction in the interrupted process, and ID_T is the maximum time the interrupt are disabled by the lower priority routine for example in critical section. When the highest –priority task interrupt one of the lower priority, the total interrupt latency is
(a) $P_T + \max(IC_T, ID_T)$
(b) $ID_T + \min(IC_T, P_T)$
(c) $\mathrm{Max}(P_T, IC_T, ID_T)$
(d) $IC_T + \max(P_T, ID_T)$

20. In a real time system, if the longest instruction used takes 100 microseconds, interrupts are never disabled for more than 90 microseconds, and the propagation delays are 110 nanoseconds for all signals. Total interrupt latency is
(a) 100.11 microseconds
(b) 90.11 microseconds
(c) 200 microseconds
(d) 110 microseconds

Answer With Detailed Explanations

Test 12

1. (d)
Mutual exclusion: Only one process can execute in its critical section.
Progress: If no process is executing in its critical section. And if there exist some process that want to enter their critical sections, then only those process that are not executing in their remainder code can take participation in the decision to enter in its critical section next, and this selection can not be postponed indefinitely.
Bounded waiting: A bound on the number of times other process are allowed to enter their critical section after a process has made a request to enter its critical section and before that request is granted must exist

2. (c)
p[0] lock(m[0] ;lock(m[1] ;unlock(m[0]); unlock (m[1]);
p[1] lock(m[1] ;lock(m[0] ;unlock(m[1]); unlock (m[0]);
p[0] and p[1] are in deadlock

3. (a)
See explanation 5

4. (b)
See explanation 5

5. (b)
When a low-priority task (ϕ1) holds a resource, and a higher priority task (ϕ2) need it. ϕ2 must block until ϕ1 relinquishes the resource. Now consider the same scenario with the addition of task ϕ3, which has a priority between that of ϕ1 and ϕ2 (fig 1 a). Because ϕ2 is blocked, ϕ3 is the highest priority ready task and will preempt ϕ1 (fig 1 b) .As a result, ϕ2 remains blocked until ϕ3 either completes or blocks, and then ϕ1 runs and frees the resources. Priority inheritance or priority lending can solve this problem. When a higher-priority task blocks on a resource, lower priority task priority is raised equal to priority of higher priority task. Thus, ϕ1 inherits the priority of ϕ2, and hence cannot be preempted by ϕ3 (fig 1(c). When ϕ1 release the resource, its priority returns to its original value, allowing ϕ2 to preempt it. ϕ3 will be scheduled only after ϕ1 has released the resource and ϕ2 has run and relinquished the CPU.

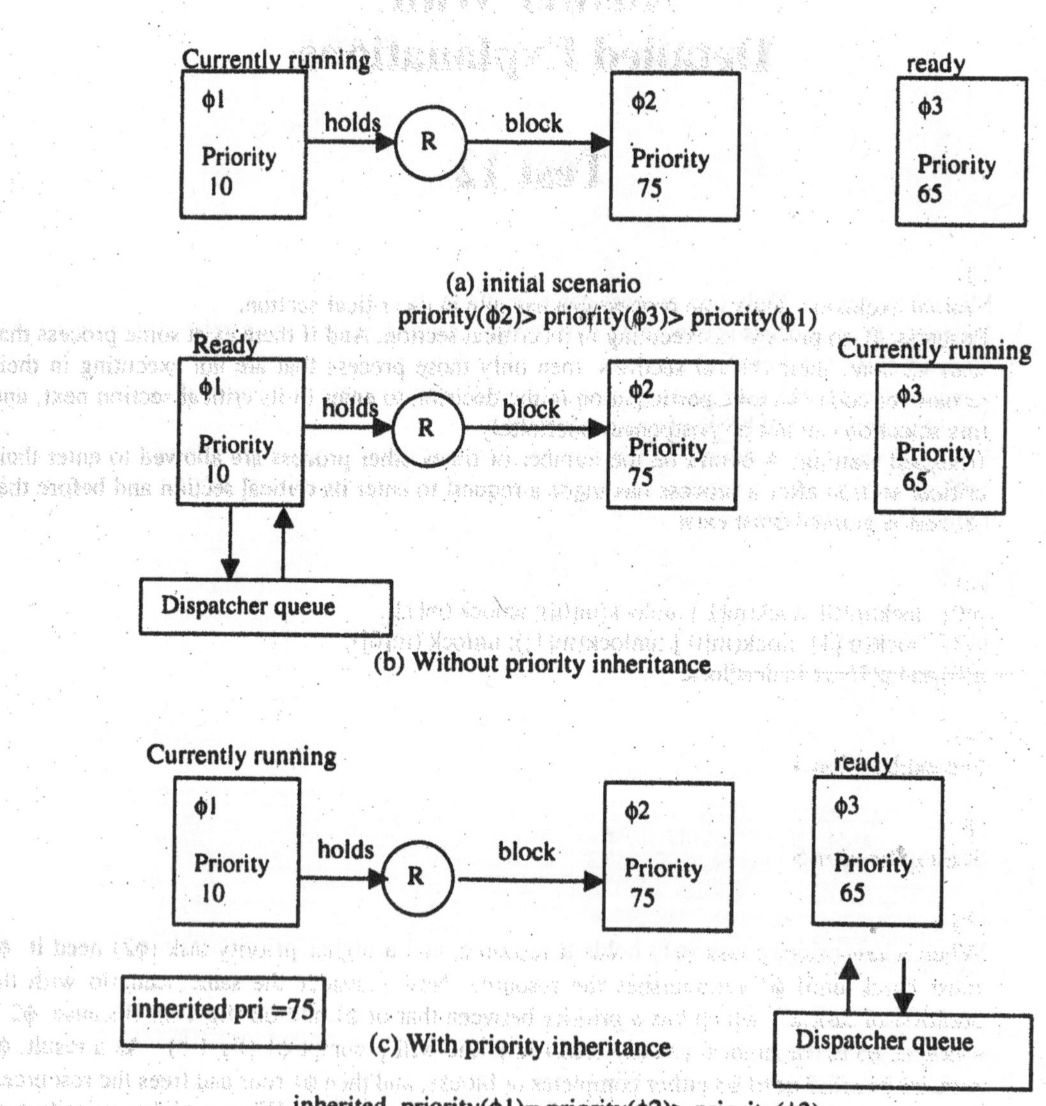

Figure 1

6. (d)

Semaphore is not owned by a specific task, because a semaphore can give multiple tasks simultaneously access to share resources. This means priority inheritance can not be implemented for semaphore;, the operating system can not check whether a task releasing a semaphore ever waited on it. Therefore any task can increment a semaphore's count by releasing it, even if the task never waited on the semaphore. A mutex object can be owned by only one task at a time

7. (d)

A dead lock situation occur if and only if the following conditions hold simultaneously
Mutual exclusion:. Only one process at a time can use the resource.
Hold and wait: There must exist a process that is holding at least one resource and is waiting to acquire additional resources that are currently held by other processes.
No preemption: Resources can not be preempted.
Circular wait: A circular wait queue must exist with two or more processes, each of them is waiting for resources held by the next process in the queue

8. (a)

When the program executes critical section, the priority structure is suspended, and the task that is executing becomes highest priority task. Thus a low priority task may become, for some duration the highest priority in the system. If no high priority task become ready during this time, there is no problem. However if a high priority task arises, the corresponding external event would not cause an immediate interrupt, and the high priority task would be delayed while the lower priority task executes. This is priority inversion. Critical section are also needed to guarantee data integrity in program using shared memory

9. (b)

Let two-process p1(higher priority) and p2(lower priority) use two critical section CS1 and CS2. These process require critical section in the following sequence

Process p1	process p2
lock CS1	lock CS2
lock CS2	lock CS1
unlock CS2	unlock CS1
unlock CS1	unlock CS2

p2 tries to lock CS1 it cannot do since p1 Has lock on it

p1 attempts to lock CS2 but blocked Because p2 has not finished it p2 which Now inherits the priority of t1 start executing

p1 locks for CS 1

p1 initiated and preempts t2 Owing to its higher priority

p2 lock for CS2

p2 start execution

t0 t1 t2 t3 t4

Priority ceiling protocol: priority ceiling of a semaphore is the highest priority of any task that may lock it. Let pri(p) denote the priority of process p , and pri(cs) the priority ceiling of the semaphore of critical section CS
consider process p1 , p2 , p3

Process	priority
p1	90 (higest)
p2	70
p3	60 (lowest)

Three critical section CS1 CS2, CS3 following table show which process may lock which critical section and resulting priority ceiling

Critical section	used by	priority ceiling
CS1	p2 p3	pri(p2)
CS2	p1 p3	pri(p1)
CS3	p3	pri(p3)

Priority inheritance protocol is similar to priority ceiling except that a process can also be blocked from entering a critical section if there exists any semaphore currently held by some other task whose priority ceiling is greater than or equal to the priority of p1.
The priority ceiling protocol prevents deadlocks
Consider above example suppose p2 currently locks CS2 and any process p1 having highest priority is initiated will be blocked from entering CS1 because its priority is not greater than the priority ceiling of CS2

10. (c)
A delay when an interrupt (events) occurs and when the CPU begins reacting to is called the interrupt latency. Mathematically it can be defined as

$$\mathbf{int_{lat} = (r_t + p_t + d_t)}$$

int_{lat} is interrupt latency
r_t the time it takes the CPU to recognize interrupt
p_t time to process an interrupt request ,
d_t Dispatch time needed by the operating system before it transfer control to your ISR
Worst case interrupt latency for device A is where device D interrupt first, then C, then B, then A
ISR for B, C and D determine how long they leave interrupt disabled to determine how long A will have to wait for its interrupt request to get processed.

11 (c)
Priority driven scheduling have been widely used in uniprocessor and multi-processor computing systems. A priority scheme is ***static*** if a priority is assigned to a task only once, while a ***dynamic*** scheme allows changing the priority with time. An example of a scheme that can be either static or dynamic is the rate –monotonic priority scheme. In this scheme, each task assigned with a priority that reflects its frequency (or request rate). The higher the task frequency (request rate) the higher is the priority assigned to the task request .If this assignment is static, then for a feasible schedule of n task on a single processor

$$\sum_{i=1}^{n} c_i f_i <= 1$$

12. (a)
Banker's algorithm are used in deadlock avoidance

13 (d)
Swapping is not suitable for real time because access time to the secondary store increase response delay
Overlays is not suitable for real time because overlays swapping from secondary storage increase response delay
MFT is not desirable in real –time operating system because its uses memory inefficiently as a result of the overhead associated with fitting a process to available memory and disk swapping
MVT is useful when the number of real –time tasks is unknown or can vary

14. (d)
See explanation 20

15 (d)
A single copy of code executed by multiple tasks and will always works correctly is called reentrant code For example, many task may call sprintf(), but there is only a single copy of the subroutine in the system.

Rules to decide if a function is reentrant or not

(1) A reentrant function may not use variable in a non-atomic way unless they are stored on the stack of the task/process that called the function or are other wise the private variable of that task/process

(2) A reentrant function may not call any other function that are not themselves reentrant

(3) A reentrant function may not use the hardware in a non-atomic way

16. This function is not reentrant for the following reason.
Violation of rule 1: Global variable j is in a fixed location in memory and therefore shared by any task that calls f .The use of j is not atomic, because the RTOS might switch tasks between the time it is tested and the time that it is updated.
May violate rule 2 for this function to be reentrant, printf must also be reentrant

17. (b)
The total memory loading is typically the sum of the individual memory loading for the program, stack and RAM area that is
$m_t = m_P \ {}^*p_P + m_r \ {}^*p_r + m_l \ {}^*p_s$
Where m_t is the total memory loading, m_p, m_r and m_s are the memory loading for the program, RAM and stack areas respectively and p_p, p_r, p_s are percentage of toatl memory allocated for the program , RAM and stack areas respectively
mt= 0.70 *50/100 + .30 * 30/100 + .60 *10/100 = 50/100 =50%

18 (d)
For device D the worst case is when all four devices interrupts simultaneously (because A, B and C, having a higher priority are processed before D. D may have to wait for ISR for A, B and C run to complete

19. (a)
P_T +max(IC_T , ID_T)
Since the interrupt will occur either while the interrupt are explicitly disabled during an instruction or when they are not, the latency is dependent on the greater of the two plus propagation delay

20. (a)
There is a delay between when an interrupt (events) occurs and when the CPU begins reacting to it; is delay is called the interrupt latency. Mathematically it can be defined as

$$int_{lat} = (r_i + p_{i} + d_i)$$

int_{lat} is interrupt latency
r_i the time it takes the CPU to recognize interrupt
p_i time to process an interrupt request ,
d_i Dispatch time needed by the operating system before it transfer control to your ISR
Suppose P_T is the interrupt latency due to propagation delay of the interrupt signal IC_T is the longest completion time for current instruction in the interrupted process, and ID_T is the maximum time the interrupt are disabled by the lower priority routine for example in critical section. When the higest –priority task interrupt one of the lower priority, the total interrupt latency is

$$P_T + \max(IC_T , ID_T) = .11 + \max(100, 90) = 100.11$$

Test 13

1. If there are two tasks $\phi 1$ and $\phi 2$, tasks are RM (rate monotonic) schedule if
   (a) $e1/T1 + e2/T2 <= 2(\sqrt{2} - 1)$
   (b) $e1/T1 + e2/T2 >= 2(\sqrt{2} - 1)$
   (c) $e1/T1 + e2/T2 <= 4(\sqrt{4} - 1)$
   (d) $e1/T1 + e2/T2 >= 4(\sqrt{4} - 1)$
   Where e1 is execution time of task ϕi and Ti is period of task ϕi.

2. Any set of n periodic tasks that fully utilizes the processor under RM must have a processor utilization of at least
   (a) $n(2^n - 1)$
   (b) $n(2^{2*n} - 1)$
   (c) $2^{1/n} - 1$
   (d) $n(2^{1/n} - 1)$

3. A process needs s/w interrupt to
   (a) Test the interrupt system of the processor
   (b) Implement coroutine
   (c) Obtain system services that need execution of privileged instruction
   (d) Return from subroutine

4. Which of the following does not interrupt a running process
   (a) A device
   (b) Power failure
   (c) Schedule process
   (d) Timer

5. Consider peterson algorithm for mutual exclusion between two concurrent process Pi and Pj the program executed by process i is shown below

```
repeat
flag[i] = true;
rotate = j;
while(S1)  do no op;
critical sections
flag[i] = false;
perform other non cs
until false;
```

   for the program to guarantee mutual exclusion, the predicate S1 in the while loop should be
   (a) flag[j] = true and rotate =I
   (b) flag[j] = true and rotate =j
   (c) flag[i] = true and rotate =j
   (d) flag[i] = true and rotate =i

6. Which of the following is false
   (a) Semaphore can't be used in an ISR;
   (b) ISR can be preempted by another ISR;
   (c) An ISR may be reentrant
   (d) Semaphore can be used in an ISR;

7. For implementation of multi-user, multi programming operating system hardware must support
   (a) Address translation
   (b) DMA for disk
   (c) At least two mode of CPU execution (privilege and non privilege)
   (d) All of the above

8. Which of the following action are typically not performed by the operating system when switching context from process P1 to process P2
   (a) Changing address translation table
   (b) Saving current register values and restoring saved register values for process b
   (c) Swapping out the main memory image of process to the disk
   (d) None of the above

9 RAID configuration of disk are used to provide
   (a) Fault tolerance
   (b) High speed
   (c) High data density
   (d) None of the above

10. Unresolved module generated by assembler that contain unresolved external references are resolved for two or more object modules by a /an
   (a) Loader
   (b) Linker
   (c) Operating system
   (d) Compiler

11. Consider a job-scheduling problem with four tasks $\phi 1$, $\phi 2$, $\phi 3$ and $\phi 4$ with corresponding deadlines
   (d1, d2 d3 ,d4) = (5,3,5,3)
   Which of the following is not a feasible solution to the problem of the scheduling the jobs without violating any job deadline
   (a) $\phi 2$, $\phi 4$, $\phi 1 \phi 3$
   (b) $\phi 4$, $\phi 2$, $\phi 1$, $\phi 3$
   (c) $\phi 4$, $\phi 1$, $\phi 2$, $\phi 3$
   (d) $\phi 2$, $\phi 4$, $\phi 3$, $\phi 1$,

12. Which of the following is false
   (a) Segmentation suffers from external fragmentation

(b) Paging suffers from internal fragmentation
(c) Segmented memory can not be paged
(d) Paging suffers from external fragmentation

13. Imposing a linear order on all resource type, each processes request resources in increasing order of enumeration is an example of
(a) Deadlock avoidance
(b) Deadlock prevention where circular waits for resources can never take place
(c) Deadlock detection
(d) None of the above

14. In segmentation, if there are 128 segments, and the maximum segments size is of 1024 words, the length of logical address is
(a) 16 bits
(b) 17 bits
(c) 18 bits
(d) 19 bits

15. Consider the following statement:
S1: Spooling is most beneficial in a multiprogramming environment where most jobs are CPU bound
S2 : Spooling is most beneficial in a multiprogramming environment where most jobs are I/O bound
(a) Only S1 is correct
(b) Only S2 is correct
(c) Both S1 and S2 are correct
(d) Both S1 and S2 are incorrect

16. Which operation require the most memory access
(a) Branch
(b) Conditional –code test
(c) Shift register right
(d) All are same

17. Consider following statement (rem)
S1: the major disadvantage of priority driven system is absence of explicit time notion in the control and management structure
S2: in priority driven system task can impose priorities that may affect the behavior of the whole system
Which of the following is true?
(a) Only S1 is correct
(b) Only S2 is correct
(c) Both S1 and S2 are true
(d) Both S1 and S2 are false

18. Gradually increasing the priority of jobs that wait in the system for a long time to remedy indefinite blocking is called
    (a) Deadlock
    (b) Aging
    (c) Starvation
    (d) Livelock

19. Which of the following is false
    (a) Non –preemptive process reduce context switching overhead and improve cache performance and pipeline performance
    (b) Non preemptive process increases context switch overhead and improves cache performance and pipeline performance
    (c) Preemptive processes increase context switches overhead and reduce cache performance
    (d) None of the above

20. Which of the following is true
    (a) A RTOS (real-time Operating System) has to be multi-threaded and preemptible.
    (b) Priority inheritance has to exist
    (c) RTOS Behavior should be known
    (d) All of the above

Answer With Detailed Explanations

Test 13

1. (a)
For RM (rate monotonic) scheduling of two task $e1/T1 + e2/T2 <= 2(\sqrt{2} - 1)$.

2. (d)
Any set of n periodic tasks that fully utilizes the processor under RM must have a processor utilization of at least $n(2^{1/n} - 1)$

3. (c)
A process needs s/w interrupt to obtain system services that need execution of privileged instruction

4. (b)

5. (b)
in order to enter the critical section, process Pi first set flag [i] to be true, and then declare that it is the other process's turn to enter if (rotate =j). If both process try to enter critical section at the same time, rotate will be set to both i and j at roughly the same time. Only one of these assignments will last; the other will occur, but be immediately overwritten. The final values of rotate decides which of the two process is allowed to enter its critical section first

6 (d)
An ISR can be preempted only by another ISR. Semaplure can't be used in an ISR; it's not possible for an ISR to block indefinitely, waiting for a resource to be available. An ISR is reentrant. While the ISR is handling an interrupt, the same interrupt can occur again and the ISR can process the second occurrence of the interrupt before it has completed processing the first software. ISR are often written to be reentrant

7. (d)
Address translation require to give different address space to different process and users
DMA is required for disk data transfer
Mode prevent errant user from harming one another

8. (c)
In context switching Os save current register values of process P1 and restore saved register value for process P2
Address translation tables are changed and new ones for the incoming process are loaded

9. (a)
Provide redundancy of data stored in the disk and thus improve fault tolerance

10. (b)
Linker is a program that accepts object modules as input, resolve external references, and produces a single output module ready for loading.

11. (c)
Both job ϕ2, ϕ4 must be scheduled by time 3, c has job sequence ϕ4, ϕ1, ϕ2, ϕ3 which violates the dead line for job ϕ2 since it is not schedule until time 3.

12. (d)
Paging suffer only internal fragmentation

13. (b)
Linear ordering on resource request makes circular waits condition impossible

14. (b)
In segmentation logical address consist
Segment number and offset into segment
For 128 segments, we need 7 bits to indicate segments from 0 to 127 (since $2^7 = 128$). In order to have space for the offset into the segment for the maximum segment size, we need at least 10 bits (since 210 = 1024) thus, length of logical address is 7+10 = 17 bits.

15. (d)
An I/O bound process is one that spends most of time doing I/O computation. A CPU bound process is one that spends more time of its time doing computation Spooling overlaps the computation of a job with the input – output of other jobs in the system. If most jobs are CPU – bound, the I/O waiting queue will be empty and system will be unbalanced. If most jobs are I/O bound the, ready queue will almost be empty, and jobs will be experienced queuing delays waiting for I/O buffers. In brief for the best performance system should have a combination of CPU –bound and I/O bound processes.

16. (d)

17. (c)
Real time operating system support a rich set of time services, as well as modern approach for task management, interrupts handling, synchronization, and communication. Some characteristics of this system are

- The system support preemptive priority scheduling, ISR is fast and predictable
- Message communication through mailbox structure and queue
- Time management is local, in the sense that the local clock dictates the knowledge of time.

Although various distribution issue along with fault tolerance issue are not addressed by these system, from the above characteristics one can see that the explicit notion of time in resource allocation and execution decision is still absent

18. (b)

19. (b)
Non –preemptive process reduce context switching overhead and improve cache performance and pipeline performance

20 (d)

Test 14

1. The principle of locality of references justifies the use of
   (a) Interrupts
   (b) Polling
   (c) Virtual memory
   (d) Cache memory

2. The portion of the process scheduler in an operating systems that dispatches process is concerned with
   (a) Assigning ready process to the CPU
   (b) Actively suspended CPU bound process
   (c) Actively suspended all process
   (d) None of the above

3. Which is the correct definition of a valid process transition within an operationg system
   (a) wake up : ready -> running
   (b) block : ready -> blocked
   (c) dispatch : ready -> running
   (d) None of the above

4. Working set theory of programming behavior of process running within an operating system involves
   (a) Assigning the process to CPU
   (b) a process scheduling mechanism
   (c) The collection of pages a process access
   (d) None of the above

5. Page fault frequency in an operating system is reduced when
   (a) Process is CPU bound
   (b) Process is I/O bound
   (c) Principal of locality is applicable to process
   (d) Size of page is reduced

6. Which of the following is true about associative memory.
   (a) the address of the data is supplied by the user
   (b) the address of the data is generated by the CPU
   (c) No need for address the data is used as an address
   (d) none of the above)

7. On receiving an interrupt from an external device the CPU
   (a) hands over control of address bus and data bus to the interrupting dvice
   (b) branches off to the interrupt service routine immediately

(c) branches off to the interrupt service routine after completion of the current instruction
(d) None of the above

8. consider a system having m resources of the same type these resources are shared by 3 process p , q , r . who have peak demand of 3 ,4 and 5 respectively. For what value of m deadlock will not occur
(a) 7
(b) 9
(c) 10
(d) 12

9. Assume that following jobs are to be executed on a single processor system (real time fencing)

job id	cpu burst time
a	4
b	4
c	2

Jobs are assumed to have arrived 0^+. Calculate the departure time (completion time) for job a if the schedule is RR with time slice 1
(a) 8
(b) 6
(c) 9
(d) 10

10. Which scheduling policy is most suitable for a time-shared OS.
(a) shortest job first
(b) round robin
(c) first come first serve
(d) Elevator

11. The process state transition diagram in figure representation of
(a) An os with a preemptive scheduling
(b) An os with a non –premptive scheduling
(c) A batch os
(d) None of the above

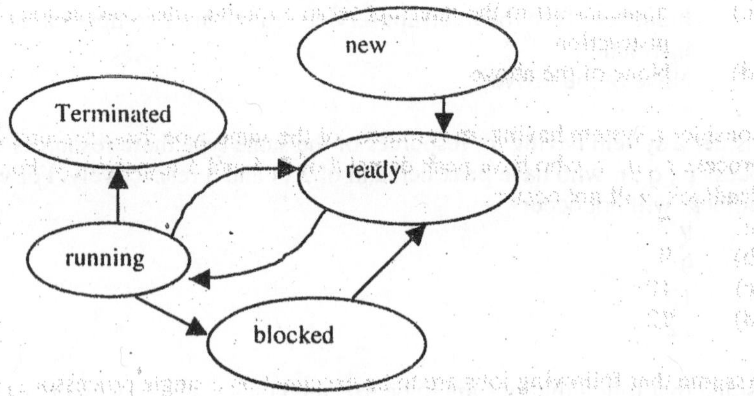

12. A critical section is a program segment
(a) which should run in a certain specified amount of time
(b) which avoid starvation
(c) which avoid deadlock
(d) where shared resources are accessed

13. Which of the following is false?
(a) The general-purpose binary semaphore is capable of addressing the requirements of both forms of task coordination: mutual exclusion and synchronization
(b) The binary semaphore has the maximum overhead associated with it, so it is not particularly applicable to high-performance requirements.
(c) The mutual-exclusion semaphore is also a binary semaphore, but it has been optimized to address problems inherent to mutual exclusion.
(d) Alternatively, the binary semaphore can be used for mutual exclusion if the advanced features of the mutual-exclusion semaphore are deemed unnecessary.

14. In a program written in c find major and minor cycle(rem)

```
main( )
{
   while(1) {
   proc_w();
   proc_x();
   proc_w();
   proc_y();
   proc_w();
   proc_x();
   proc_w();
   proc_z();
}
```

15. Assume we have seven resources R1, R2, ...R7, and among them R1, R2, R3 are active resources. Let current EAT (earliest available time) be
EAT =(EAT1, EAT2, EAT3, EAT4, EAT5, EAT6, EAT7)
(3 10, 25, 15, 10, 15, 3)
And let task T with computation time C = 5, and with resources requirements R1, R2, and R5, be one of the tasks that remain to be scheduled
Start time S (T) for task T is
(a) 5
(b) 10
(c) 15
(d) None of the above

16 New EAT is
(a) (5 , 20 , 25 , 15, 10 ,15,5)
(b) (20 , 20 , 25 , 15, 10 ,15,5)
(c) (15 , 15 , 25,15,15,15,5)
(d) (5 , 10 , 25 , 15, 10 ,15,5)

17 Consider the case of scheduling of two task $\phi 1$ and $\phi 2$ .Let T1 and T2 be the request periods f the tasks, with T1 =2 , T2 =5 and their run time being C1=1 , C2=2. For feasible task chedule
(a) $\phi 1$ be the higher priority task
(b) $\phi 2$ be the higher priority task
(c) Priority of $\phi 1$ be equl to priority of $\phi 2$
(d) Not depend on priority

18. For a feasible schedule the value of C2 can be increased at most to
(a) 6
(b) 3
(c) 2
(d) 5

19. Suppose P_T is the interrupt latency due to propagation delay of the interrupt signal IC_T is the longest completion time for current instruction in the interrupted process, and ID_T is the maximum time the interrupt are disabled by the lower priority routine for example in critical section. When the lowest –priority task interrupt one of the higher priority interrupt, the total interrupt latency is
(a) Time to complete higher priority routine
(b) Max (P_T ,IC_T , ID_T)
(c) IC_T +max(P_T , ID_T)
(d) None of the above

20. An OS makes uses of dijstrea ' banker's algorithm to allocate 8 memory buffers. Memory buffers will be allocated to a task requesting them only if there are enough available memory buffers to allow it tio run to completion. there are three user using memory buffer. user 1 is

using 3 memory buffers and will need at most 7 memory buffers . user 2 is using 1 memory buffers and will need at most 4 memory buffers. User 3 is using two memory buffers and will need at most 4 memory buffers memory buffers . each user is currently requesting one more memory buffers . which of the following is true

(a) the os will grant a memory buffer to user 1 only
(b) the os will grant a memory buffer to user 2 only
(c) the os will grant a memory buffer to user 3 only
(d) none of the above

Answer With Detailed Explanations

Test 14

1. (d)
Locality of references means that many instructions in each of a few localized areas of the program are repeatedly executed, while the remaining part of the program is accessed relatively infrequently. Hence, the use of cache, a high speed memory, to hold these localized areas can improve the performance

2. (a)

3. (c)

4. (c)

5. (c)
principle of locality says that a process tends to access data within a small area of memory therefore , request across page boundaries will be reduced , so page faults will occur less frequently

6. (c)
associative memory is known as content address memory, CAM . that is , the data are addressed by the data itself.

7. (c)
when interrupt occur cpu complete current instruction ten transfer control to interrupt service routine

8. (d)
total peak demand 3+4+5 = 12

9. (c)

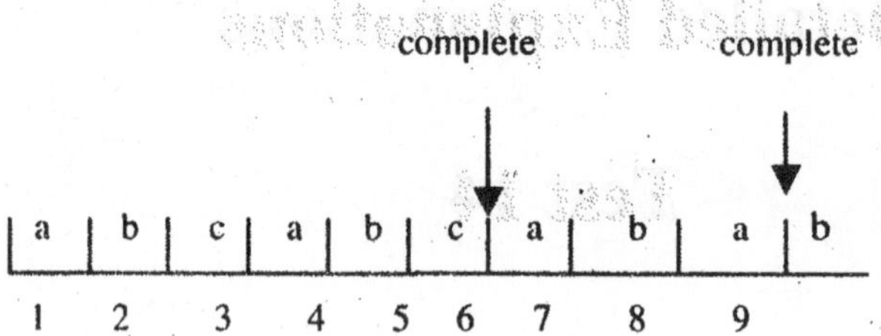

10. (b)

11. (a)

12. (d)

13. (b)
The binary semaphore has the least overhead associated with it, making it particularly applicable to high-performance requirements.

14. major cycle wxwywxwz
minor cycle wxwz wxwy wx wy wz
If the scheduling of task is shown on a time line and if the assignment uses rate-monotonic discipline, then scheduling sequence repeats itself after a certain period of time. This sequence is called a major cycle, smaller sequence also repeat they are called minor cycles.

15 (b)
Since a task T can run only when all the resources it needs are available we define ST(T) as
S(T) = MAX(EAT I where T needs Ri)
S(T) = MAX(EAT1, EAT2, EAT5)
MAX(3, 10 , 10) = 10

16 (c)
For a given feasible schedule to remain feasible when extended by T
ST(T) + C(T) <= D(T) (where C is computation time and D is deadline)
Must hold
Now new EAT(T) is
NEW_EAT(T) = (15 , 15 , 25,15,15,15,5)
Because T is assumed to start at its ST and it uses ten units of computation time while holding R1 ,R2 and R5.

17. (a)
T1=2 T2= 5

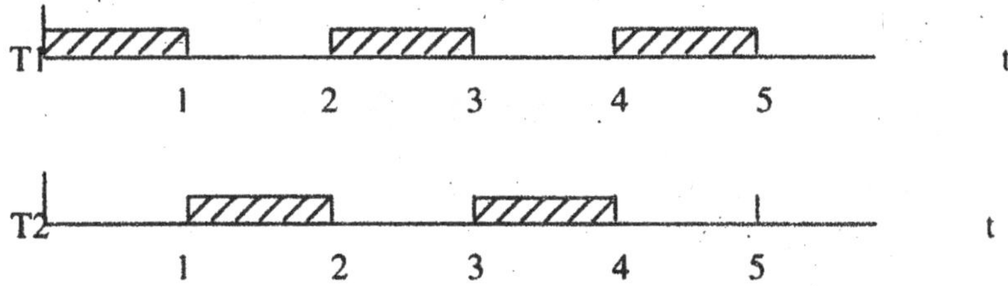

from figure it it can be see that value of C2 can be increased at most to 2 but not further When $\phi 2$ be the higher priority task , then neither of the values of C1 and C2 can be increased beyond one.

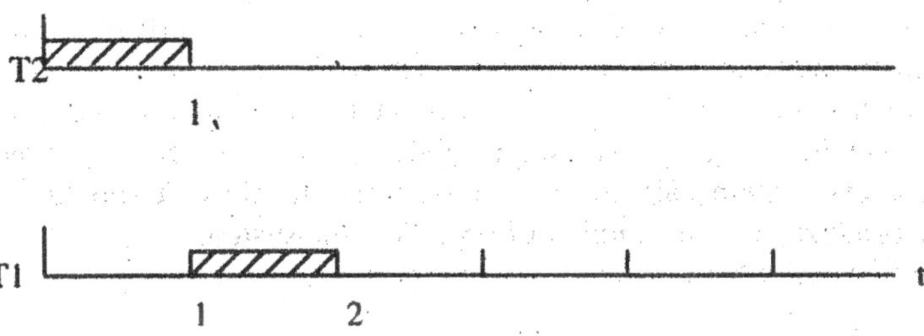

18 (c)
see explanation 24

19. (a)

20 (c)

	No of memory buffers in use	Number of memory buffer needed
user 1	3	7
use 2	1	4
user 3	2	4

No of memory buffers available (8 –6 = 2) user 1 and user 2 will not bbe granted memory buffers because they will need more than two memory buffers to run to completion . user 3 will be granted one memory buffer , another one is available later for it to complete and then reliquish all four memory buffers . now 4 memory buffers are available and three memory buffers can be allocated to , say , user 2 so that it completes . now five memory buffer s are available three can be allocated to user 1 so that it completes , thus no deadlock occurs

FAQ on Embedded System Programming

Test 15

Q1. What makes an OS a RTOS?

A1.
- A RTOS (real-time Operating System) has to be multi-tasking and pre-emptible
- task priority has to exist.
- Behavior of OS should be known.
- OS should support predictable task synchronization mechanisms
- A system of priority inheritance has to exist.

So the following parameter should be clearly specified by the RTOS manufacturer:
The interrupt latency (i.e. time from interrupt to task run), this has to be compatible with application requirements and has to be predictable. This value depends on the number of simultaneous pending interrupts. Example QNX real-time OS Interrupt Latency is 4.4µsec
- For every system call, the maximum times it takes. It should be predictable and independent from the number of objects in the system;
- The maximum time the OS and drivers mask the interrupts.

Q2. What are differences among hardware interrupt software interrupt and exceptions?

A2. Fundamental differences between hardware and software interrupt are the trigger mechanism. The trigger of a hardware interrupt is an electrical signal from a external devices. The trigger of a software interrupt is the execution of a machine language instruction. Software interrupt execution is planned –it's an instruction (example INT 13) that the programmer wrote into the software at a specific point where as a hardware interrupt takes place asynchronously. Because a hardware interrupt is external event, its execution is an unplanned event.
An exception (frequently called a processor exception) is an interrupt that is internal to the CPU and triggered by a software program's attempt to perform an illegal operation. As with hardware and software program's attempt to perform an illegal operation. Exceptions cause a transfer of control, and the CPU responds to the exception by executing an ISR.

Q3. What are difference between software interrupts and procedure calls?

A3. An interrupt automatically preserves the processor flags; that does not happen in a procedure call. To call an ISR only interrupt number is required not memory location of the ISR, Whereas in a procedure call instruction includes the memory address of the procedure. If Processors support privileged and unprivileged (or application) mode of execution then interrupts can automatically switch the CPU to a more privileged level. Normal procedure call can't across privilege level, however, often a special procedure call instruction is provided specially for calling from application code to system code.

Q4. What happen when exception occurs at interrupt level?

A4. When a task/process cause a hardware exception such as illegal instruction, the task is suspended and the rest of the system continues uninterrupted. However, when an ISR causes such an exception, there is no safe recourse for the system to handle the exception. The ISR has no context that can be suspended instead, some RTOS(VxWorks) stores the descriptions of the exception in a special location in Low memory and executes a system restart.

Q5. What is reentrant code?

A5. In RTOS it is common for a single copy of a subroutine or subroutine library to be called by many tasks. For example, many task may call sprintf(), but there is only a single copy of the subroutine in the system . A single copy of code executed by many tasks is called shared code. Shared code must be reentrant.

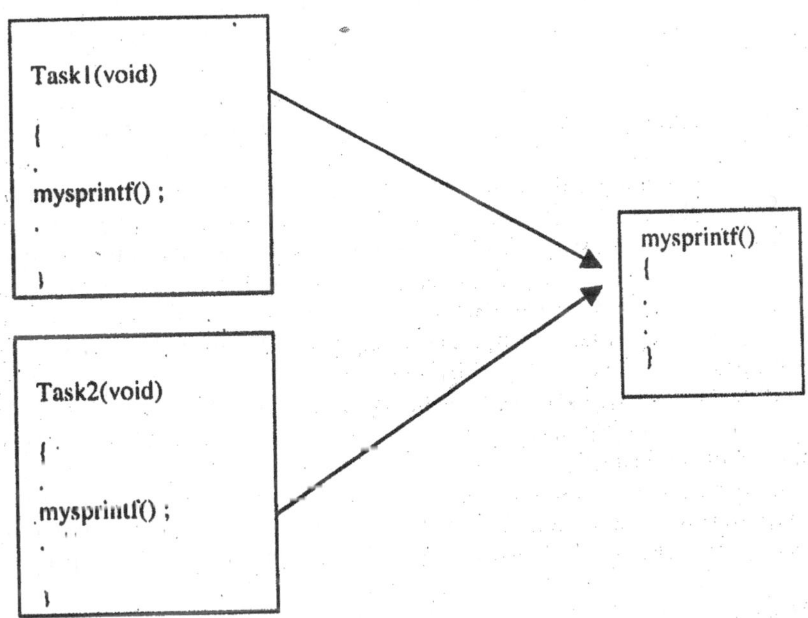

A subroutine is reentrant if a single copy of the routine can be called from many task simultaneously without conflict. Such conflict occurs due to share of global or static variables, because there is only a single copy of the data and code. A subroutine access to such a variable can overlap and interfere in invocations from different task contexts.

Q6. What is interrupt latency?

A6. There is a delay between when an interrupt (events) occurs and when the CPU begins reacting to it; this delay is called the interrupt latency. Mathematically it can be defined as

$$int_{lat} = (r_t + p_t + d_t)$$

int_{lat} is interrupt latency
r_t the time it takes the CPU to recognize interrupt
p_t time to process an interrupt request ,
d_t Dispatch time needed by the operating system before it transfer control to ISR

Q7. What is a critical section?

A7. A critical section is a code segment accessing shared variables and only one process can execute at a time. Once started, must be completed without interruption, in other words, a critical section operation is individual and satisfy the following requirements

- Mutual exclusion – at most one process executing the cs at a time
- No deadlock – no circular wait by two or more process trying to enter the cs at - least one will succeed.
- Non preemption no interrupt until completion, once entered the cs
- Eventual entry A process attempting to enter its critical sections will eventually succeed

Q8. Define multiprogramming, multiprocessing, multitasking, multithreading.

A8. Multiprogramming is defined as multiple independent programs running on a single processor or on a multiprocessor by time–sharing use of the system resources. A multiprogrammed, multiprocessor allows multiple programs to run concurrently through time sharing of all the processor in the system. Multiple program are interleaved in their CPU and I/O activities when a program is in I/O mode the processor switches to another program.
Multiprocessing: when multiprogramming is implemented at the process level on a multiprocessor, it is called multiprocessing.
Multitasking a single program can be partitioned into multiple interrelated tasks concurrently executed on a multiprocessor. Multitasking provides the simultaneous execution of two or more parts of a single program.
Multithreading is an extension of the concepts of multitasking and multiprocessing. The purpose is to exploit parallelism in modern multiprocessor built with multiple context processors with multiple instruction issues each thread may use a separate program counter.

Q9. What is spin lock?

A9. Entrance and exit of a *critical section* can be controlled by a binary spin lock mechanism in which the gate is protected by a single binary variable x, which is shared by all process attempting to enter the CS.
binary spin lock
The gate variable x is initially set 0, corresponding to *open* status each process Pi is allowed to test the value of x until it becomes 0 then it can enter the CS .The gate must be closed by setting x =1 after entering

```
Enum shared{ 1,0};
```

```
Shared x    ;            // the spin lock
x= 0   ;            // the cs is open  initially
Process Pi for all  i
do
{.
..                     // spinning with busy wait
..
}while( x!=0)
x:=1;               // close gate after entry
;;
;;
//                     the  critical section
x:=0;               / open  gate after done  and exit
```

Q10. Define binary semaphore and counting semaphore.

A10. A binary semaphore is a Boolean variable taking the values of 1 an 0. Each shared resources or CS can be associated with a dedicated semaphore. Only two atomic operation, P and V are used to access the CS represented by the semaphore apart from initialization by setting x =1 the P(x) operation causes the values of the semaphore to be decreased by 1 if x is not already 0

The V(x) operation cause the value of the semaphore to be increased by 1 if x is not already 1

x=1 means the resource is available represented by x

x=0 means the resources is being occupied

A counting semaphore x is a nonnegative integer taking (n+1) possible values 0,1,2…,n . a binary semaphore is a special case of n=1. A counting semaphore with a maximum values of n represent availability of n copies of shared resources

A shared resources can be a program segment, buffer or i/o .P(x) and V(x) on counting semaphore is defined as

- P(x) : if(x>0) then x=x-1 ; else suspended the execution of the current and put it in a wait queue
- V(x) : if the wait queue is not empty , then wakeup one of them ; else x=x+1

P(X) means submission of a request for a permit

V(x) means return of permit after a process finishes using a copy of the resources

Q11. Define mutual exclusion semaphore.

A11. The mutual –exclusion semaphore is a specialized binary semaphore to address issues inherent in mutual exclusion, including priority inversion, deletion safety and recursive access to resources. The fundamental behavior of the mutual exclusion semaphore is identical to binary semaphore, with the following exceptions

- it can be given by the task that took it
- it can not be given from an ISR

Q12. What is a flash memory?

A12. Flash memory sometimes called flash EEPROM (Electrically erasable programmable read – only memory) is a variation of EEPROM. Flash memory retains its contents after power is off. However whereas standard EEPROM contents are read and written on a per-byte basis, flash memory contents must be modified in blocks. Flash memory is more expensive than EEPROM but can be rewritten thousands of times rather than hundreds of times.

Q13 How real-time system are distinguished from desktop application?

A13. The timeliness of a response in real –time system is a predetermined, inflexible and necessary for correct operation. In other words if a real time system not respond some events within time, the system is wrong. However, the timeliness of a response in a desktop can varies and is not necessary for correct operation. If it takes a PC a few seconds more to execute a program, the delay is acceptable. Timelines in a desktop system is important; timeliness in real –time system is critical.

Q14. Define periodic, aperiodic or sporadic task

A14. A task ϕi is periodic if it is released every Ti seconds periodically, Ti is called the period of task Ti.. The task is sporadic if it is not periodic, but may be invoked at irregular intervals. Sporadic tasks are characterized by an upper bound on the rate at which they may be invoked. Sporadic tasks are sometimes also called aperiodic.

Q15. Define task, process and thread.

A15. A task may be either a process or a thread. Basically it refers to a sequence of related computations that work together to achieve end result. for example a system may include a task to read data from a specific port, task can be implemented as a thread or as a process (or as an interrupt service routine.
A multitasking system can run multiple tasks simultaneously those task might be process, thread or both.
Process is an independent program, having its own data space and code space in memory. The data variables that a process owns is owns by itself and this is true for all process running in the system,. One process can not see the variable in another process unless that other process agrees to let it do so.
Within a process a thread is a separate execution path. Each thread shares the same code and global data but has its own private stack. Because the stack is per thread, local variables are private to each thread, to create a new thread program executes a call to the operation system that make a new thread of execution.
Process has its own global data. thread exist within process, so all the threads share the global variables of a process

Q16. How does a system respond when more than one device generates interrupt simultaneously? .

A16. CPU process interrupt with the highest priority first. Each hardware interrupts is assigned a unique priority on the CPU with multiple interrupt input pins, the priority of each interrupt is usually hardwired into the processor. When more than one interrupt occurs simultaneously, one will have the highest priority. Highest priority interrupt will be serviced first. The lower – priority interrupt are put on hold and dealt with in order of priority.

Q17. What are special limitations of ISR?

A17. The basic restriction on ISR is that they must not call blocking primitive. Example they must not try to take a semaphore, because if the semaphore is unavailable, the kernel tries to switch the caller to the Block State. However, ISR can give semaphore, releasing any tasks waiting on them. The memory facilities malloc and free take a semaphore, they can not be called by ISR, and neither can routine that make calls to malloc() and free(). For example ISR can not call any release or deletion routine in ISR, also an ISR must not call routines that use a floating –point coprocessor.

Q18. What is BSP(Board support package)

A18 To facilitate application development on customer hardware, RTOS usually provide Board support package. BSP provide a mechanism for supporting standard and custom embedded hardware designs with RTOS. BSP provides a software templates that includes skeleton device driver code and code for low level system functions that are required by particular hardware devices. The device driver code itself is specific to individual peripheral devices, but is not specific to the board the devices are on.

Q19 What is Priority inversion

A19 See explanation of Q5 (test12)

Q20 Define priority inheritance and priority ceiling protocol ceiling

A20 See explanation of Q9 (test 12)

Q21. Define hard real time and soft real time system

A21. A task is said to be real–time, if it must be completed by a deadline. Given a system of real - time process (each performing a real time task), the system must schedule them all so as to guarantee that all deadlines are met. There is some cases in which missed deadline may be tolerated as long as not too many deadline are missed or they are not missed by much this is what called soft real time system. Not meeting the deadline or missed deadline Is considered a system failure this is what called hard real time system.

Q22. Is there any difference between task and process?

A22. Tasks can address memory directly while processes cannot; and processes inherit only some specific attributes from their parent process, while tasks operate in exactly the same environment as the parent task.
Tasks and processes are alike in that they can be scheduled independently.

Q23. Show how the semaphore can be used for mutual exclusion and synchronization

A23 **Mutual Exclusion:** Binary semaphores limit the scope of the mutual exclusion to only the Associated resource. In this technique, a semaphore is created to guard the resource. Initially the Semaphore is available (full).

When a task wants to access the resource, it must first take that semaphore. As long as the task keeps the semaphore, all other tasks requesting access to the resource are blocked from execution. When the task is finished with the resource, it release the semaphore, allowing another task to use the resource.

Accesses to a resource requiring mutual exclusion are bracketed with semTake( ) and semGive( ) pairs:

```
semTake (semMutex, WAIT_FOREVER); / vx works/
    .
    .  critical region, only accessible by a single task at a time
    .
semGive (semMutex);
```

Synchronization : as used for task synchronization, a semaphore can represent a condition or event that a task is waiting for. Initially the semaphore is unavailable (empty). A task or ISR signals the occurrence of the event by giving the semaphore

When used for mutual exclusion, the semaphore is initially full, and each task first takes, then gives back the semaphore. For synchronization, the semaphore is initially empty, and one task waits to take the semaphore given by another task.

Q24. Is semaphores are the primary means for addressing the requirements of both mutual exclusion and task synchronization.

A24. Yes, for mutual exclusion, semaphores interlock access to shared resources. They provide mutual exclusion with finer granularity than either interrupt disabling or preemptive locks, For synchronization, semaphores coordinate a task's execution with external events.

Q25. What is real time fencing?

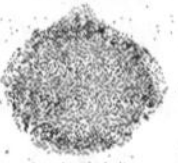

A25. A configurable priority level used to determine which task would be time-sliced

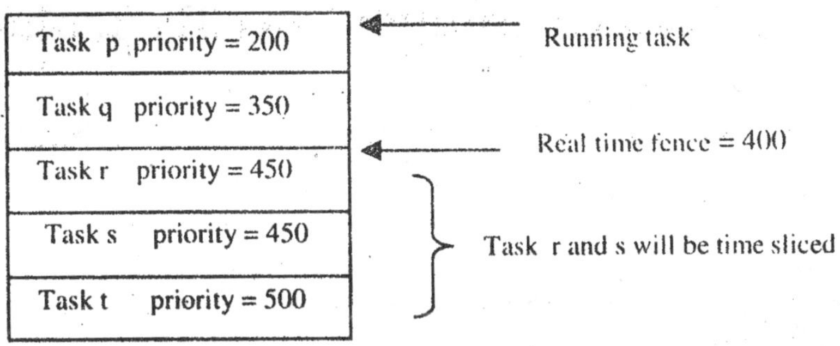

Ready queue

Appendix A
Implementation specific problem

The order in which the operand of an operator are evaluated is not specified except following operator
&&
||
?:
,
Function call, ++ operator and – -operator cause side effect
Function call,
Consider the problem

```
main( )
{
    int a[][3] = { 1,2,3 ,4,5,6};
    int (*ptr)[3] =a ;
    printf("%d %d\n "  ,(*++ptr)[1], (*ptr)[2] ); }
}
```

Can produce different result for different compiler depending on whether ptr is incremented before (*ptr)[2] or after (*ptr)[2]
++ Operator and -- operator
Consider int i =1 a[i] = i++; may be evaluated as a[1] = 1 , or a[2] =1. the subexpression i ++ causes a side effect it modifies i value that cause undefined behavior because i is also used as a subscript . Subscript can be the old value or new value that depend upon compiler interpretation
And consider the following program

```
#include<stdio.h>
main( )
{
    int j;
    int i =2 ;
    j= i ++* i++ ;
    printf("%d", j) ;
    j = ++i * ++i ;
    printf("%d" , j ) ;
    j = i-- *--i ;
    printf("%d" , j ) ;
}
```

Exact behavior of above code that contains ambiguous side affect has been undefined. A single expression should not cause the same variable to be modified twice or to be modified and then examined. Above code depends on compiler implementations

Appendix B
Use of Volatile

A variable should be declared volatile whenever its value can be changed by something beyond the control of the program in which it appears, such as a concurrently executing thread.
Volatile, can appear only once in a declaration with any type specifier; however, they cannot appear after the first comma in a multiple item declaration. For example, the following declarations are legal.
Let T denotes some data type
typedef volatile T i;
volatile T i;
T volatile i ;
and the following declaration is illegal
T i, volatile vi ;
Volatile qualifiers can be used to change the behavior of a type. For example, volatile int p = 3; declares and initializes an object with type volatile int whose value will be always read from memory.

Syntax
Keyword volatile can be placed before or after the data type in the variable definition. For example following declaration are identical:
Volatile T a =3;
T volatile a=3;
The declaration declare and initialize an objet with type volatile T whose value will be always read from memory
pointer declaration
Volatile T * ptr;
T volatile * ptr;
Ptr is a a pointer to a volatile T:
volatile pointer to a volatile variable
int volatile * volatile ptr;
volatile can be applied to derived types such as an array type ,in that case, the element is qualified, not the array type. when applied to struct types entire contents of the struct become volatile. You can apply the volatile qualifier to the individual members of the struct.
Type qualifiers are relevant only when accessing identifiers as l-values in expressions.
The following are legal volatile declarations:
T volatile *ptr_vi ; /* Pointer to volatile T */
T *volatile vptr_i; /* volatile pointer to T */
T volatile vi; /* Volatile integer */
volatile does not affects the range of values or arithmetic properties of the object.
To declare the item pointed to by the pointer as volatile, use a declaration of the form:
volatile T *vptr;
To declare the value of the pointer — that is, the actual address stored in the pointer — as volatile, use a declaration of the form:
T* volatile ptrv;

Use of volatile

- An object that is a memory-mapped I/O port
- An object variable that is shared between multiple concurrent processes
- An object that is modified by an interrupt service routine
- An automatic object declared in a function that calls setjmp and whose value is-changed between the call to setjmp and a corresponding call to longjmp

 # An object that is a memory-mapped I/O port
an 8 bit , memory –mapped I/O port at physical address 0X15 can be declared as
char const ptr=(char*)0X15 ;
*ptr access the port consider following code fragment to set the third bit of the output port at periodic intervals

```
*ptr = 0;
while(*ptr){
    *ptr = 4 ;
    *ptr = 0 ;
}
```

the above code may be optimize as

```
*ptr = 0
while(0) {
}
```

*ptr is assigned 0 before value 4 is used (and value of *ptr never changes (same constant is always assigned to it)
volatile keyword is used to suppress these optimization the compiler assumes that the value can change any time , even if no explicit code modify it
to suppress all optimization declare ptr as
volatile char * **const ptr = (volatile char*)0x16**
this declaration say the object at which ptr points can change without notice , but that ptr itself is a constant whose value never change

 # An object that is shared between multiple concurrent processes
if two threads/tasks concurrently assign distinct values to the same shared non-volatile variable, a subsequent use of that variable may obtain a value that is not equal to either of the assigned values, but some implementation dependent mixture of the two values. so a global variable ... multiple thread programmers must declare shared variable a

```
#include<thread.h>
#include<stdio.h>
volatile int num ;
void* foo()
{,
```

```
    while(1) {
        ++num ;
        sleep(1000);
        }
    }
    main()
    {
    int p ;
    void *targ =NULL ;
    thread_t id ;
    num = 0;
    p = thr_create((void*)NULL , 0,foo,targ,0,&id);
    if(!p)  printf(" can not create thread ");

    }
    while(1) {
       printf("%d" , num ) ;
       }
    }
```

the compiler may use a register to store the num variable in the main thread , so the change to the value by the second thread are ignored . The volatile modifier is a away of telling the compiler that no optimization applied to the variable its value be not placed in register and value may change outside influence during evaluation

 # An automatic object declared in a function that calls setjmp and whose value is-changed between the call to setjmp and a corresponding call to longjmp

Variables local to functions that call setjmp is most often used. When an automatic object is declared in a function that calls setjmp, the compilation system knows that it has to produce code that exactly matches what the programmer wrote. Therefore, the most recent value for such an automatic object will always be in memory (not just in a register) and as such will be guaranteed to be up-to-date when longjmp is called. Without volatile variable is undefined by the standard whether the result one see differs with or without optimization simply reflects that fact

Consider following code

```
#include<setjmp.h>
static jmp_buf  buf ;
main( )
{
   volatile  int b;
   b =3 ;
   if(setjmp(buf)!=0)  {
   printf("%d ", b) ;
   exit(0);
```

```
    }
    b=5;
    longjmp(buf , 1) ;
  }
```

volatile variable isn't affected by the optimization. So value of b is after the longjump is the last value variable assigned. Without volatile b may or may not be restored to its last value when the longjmp occurs.

 # An object modified by an interrupt service routine

Interrupt service routines often set variables that are tested in main line code. One problem that arises as soon as you use interrupt is that interrupt routines need to communicate with rest of the code .A interrupt may update a variable num that is used in main line of code .An incorrect implementation of this might be:

```
static lon int  num ;
void interrupt update(void)
{
++num ;
}
main()
{
long  val ;
val  = num ;
while(val !=num)
val = num ;
rturn val ;
}
```

When compilation system execute while statement, the optimizer in compiler may notice that it read the value num once already and that value is still in the register. Instead of re reading the value from memory, compiler may produce code to use the (possibly messed up) value in the register defeating purpose of original C program. Some compiler may optimize entire while loop assuming that since the value of num was just assigned to val , the two must be equal and condition in while statement will therefore always be false To avoid this ,you have to declare num to be volatile that warns compilers that certain variables may change because of interrupt routines.

static volatile long int num ;

With volatile keyword in the declaration the compiler knows that the value of num must b read from memory every time it is referenced.

Conclusion

If you are given a piece of touchy code given above. It is a good idea in any case to look the compiler outputting listing at the assembly language to be sure that compiler produce code that makes sense.

DATA STRUCTURE THROUGH C IN DEPTH

"Data structures through C in Depth" presents the concept of data structures in very clear and understandable manner. It covers data structures syllabus of different undergraduate and post graduate courses and can be useful for both beginners and professional programmers. This book can be used by students for self study as the concept are explained in step by step manner followed by clear and easy to comprehend complete programs. The explanation are illustrated by detailed examples, figures and tables throughout the book. Exercises with solution are provided which help in having a better understanding of the text. The CD-ROM contains all the programs given in the book. Some 'demo' programs are included in the CD which demonstrate the stepwise working of the algorithms.

Price: Rs. 360/-
ISBN:9788183337411
Pages: 525
Author: Srivastava/
Srivastava

The book explains each topic in depth without compromising over the lucidity of the text and programs. This approach makes this book suitable for both novices and advanced programmers. The well structured programs are easily understandable by the beginners and useful for the experienced programmers. The book contains about 300 programs, 210 exercises and 80 programming exercises with solutions of exercises and hints to solve programming exercises. The chapter on projects development and library creation can help students in implementing their knowledge and become a perfect C programmers.

Contents

- ✓ Introduction
- ✓ Array, Pointers And Structures
- ✓ Linked Lists
- ✓ Stacks And Queues
- ✓ Recursion
- ✓ Trees
- ✓ Graphs
- ✓ Sorting
- ✓ Searching And Hashing
- ✓ Storage Management

Available at www.bpbonline.com, Amazon, Flipkart, Paytm, and all Leading Book Stores

26082016